Praise for STORIES ABOUT MY FIRST CHURCH

I laughed at the story of Elmer Towns riding his bicycle all over Savannah, Georgia, to win people to Christ, then hiding the bike behind the hospital because he wanted people to think he was as sophisticated as the other ministers. It's an outstanding book, written in honest integrity.

JERRY FALWELL

Pastor, Thomas Road Baptist Church–Lynchburg, Virginia

What fun this book was! Not only was the book a help to me (the principles at the end of each chapter are excellent), but I enjoyed seeing another side of the man I've known as Dr. Elmer Towns, nationally known educator, conference speaker and author. Just to know that Elmer Towns would ride all over Savannah on his bicycle with his pant leg rolled up to minister to his people and tell others, "You must be born again," was an encouragement to me.

DR. CARL GODWIN

Pastor, Bible Baptist Church–Lincoln, Nebraska

I ended up bursting out in laughter as I read this excellent and delightful book. It refreshed my heart, renewed my love and brought me back to the one grand focus of ministry—people. This book makes church life fun again.

TED HAGGARD

Pastor, New Life Church–Colorado Springs, Colorado

Elmer Towns has a way of addressing the significant and the timely concerns of all leaders. God bless the host of small churches that are God's instruments to envelop our culture with a work of love.

JACK W. HAYFORD, LITT.D.

Senior Pastor, The Church On The Way–Van Nuys, California

God delights when the gospel is proclaimed and souls get saved. Dr. Towns as a 19-year-old preacher proclaimed, "Ye must be born again" in and out of season from the pulpits, visitations, in funeral services and on every occasion. God honored his message and souls got saved and the church revived. Even today, Dr. Towns's main business is salvation. Whenever people greet him saying, "How are you?" Dr. Towns always replies, "I am still saved."

DR. C. DANIEL KIM

Professor, Liberty Baptist Theological Seminary

You'll smile at this personal, self-revealing story, but you will also learn that God can use any one of us beyond our abilities if we are single-mindedly devoted to Him.

DR. ERWIN W. LUTZER
Senior Pastor, The Moody Church–Chicago, Illinois

If everyone studying for church leadership would read this book, they would take themselves less seriously but take the ministry more seriously. I want every young minister to read this book because they will be better leaders.

JOHN MAXWELL
Founder, Injoy, Inc.

Like Elmer Towns, I began pastoring at the age of nineteen in a very small but gloriously wonderful rural church. What memories! This book will help every pastor of a small church to rejoice in this special treasure that is his.

ADRIAN ROGERS
Pastor, Bellevue Baptist Church–Cordova, Tennessee

This is a warmhearted and often humorous tribute to those who've heard God's call and faithfully served His flock. It encourages, inspires, challenges and entertains—all at the same time.

RICK WARREN
Pastor, Saddleback Valley Community Church

Reading Elmer Towns's new book brings back a flood of memories. I thank God for the small church, and for the lessons I learned as the pastor of more than one small country church. I will never forget those days, or the men and women whose lives shaped and sharpened mine as we grew together in the Lord.

ED YOUNG
Pastor, Second Baptist Church–Houston, Texas

FOREWORD BY JOHN MAXWELL

STORIES ABOUT
MY FIRST
CHURCH

※ *Who Stole the Bride?* ※

※ *Let's Paint the Church in One Day* ※

※ *There's No Toilet Paper* ※

※ *The Man Who Saw Jesus* ※

{ AND OTHER STORIES ABOUT GOD'S GRACE AND
GUIDANCE IN THE LIFE OF A YOUNG PASTOR }

Elmer L. Towns

Regal

A Division of Gospel Light
Ventura, California, U.S.A.

Published by Regal Books
A Division of Gospel Light
Ventura, California, U.S.A.
Printed in U.S.A.

Regal Books is a ministry of Gospel Light, an evangelical Christian publisher dedicated to serving
the local church. We believe God's vision for Gospel Light is to provide church leaders with biblical, user-friendly materials that will help them evangelize, disciple and minister to children, youth
and families.

It is our prayer that this Regal book will help you discover biblical truth for your own life and help
you meet the needs of others. May God richly bless you.

For a free catalog of resources from Regal Books/Gospel Light please contact your Christian supplier or call
1-800-4-GOSPEL.

Library of Congress Cataloging-in-Publication Data
Towns, Elmer L.
    Stories about my first church / Elmer L. Towns.
        p. cm.
    ISBN 0-8307-1890-7 (hardcover)
    1. Towns, Elmer L. 2. Baptists—United States—Clergy—Biography. 3. Presbyterian Church—United
States—Biography. 4. Westminster Presbyterian Church (Savannah, Ga.) 5. Clergy—Office. 6. Pastoral the-
ology. 7. Savannah (Ga.)—Church history—20th century.
    I. Title.
    BX6495.T597A3 1997
    286.1'092—dc21
    [B]
                                    96-46206
                                       CIP

1 2 3 4 5 6 7 8 9 10 11 12 13 14 15 / 03 02 01 00 99 98 97

Rights for publishing this book in other languages are contracted by Gospel Literature International
(GLINT). GLINT also provides technical help for the adaptation, translation and publishing of Bible
study resources and books in scores of languages worldwide. For further information, contact GLINT,
P.O. Box 4060, Ontario, CA 91761-1003, U.S.A., or the publisher.

To

Silla Hair, one woman who made a difference,

and

to the exceptional people of the Westminster Presbyterian Church who followed my leadership, misapplying the verse, "A child shall lead them." Just as most grown men never forget their first date, first kiss and first love, I will never forget this congregation. These people will always have a special place in my heart.

Special thanks to

Eddie Dearing, the son of Silla Hair, who read the manuscript for accuracy and supplied dates and names I forgot.

Rev. Cecil Hodges, who supplied information about how the people of Westminster Presbyterian Church became members of his Baptist church.

Dr. Earl McQuay and Rev. Herb Dickinson, who read for accuracy the accounts of their involvement in the church.

Contents

Foreword by John Maxwell —·—·—·—·—·—·—·—·—·—·— 9

Introduction: Why a 19-Year-Old Pastor? —·—·—·—·—·— 11

1. The Key to My First Pastorate —·—·—·—·—·—·—·— 13
   An unusual call to an unusual candidate to pastor an
   unusual church—all because five ladies had the key.

2. Painting the Whole Church in a Whole Day —·—·— 25
   Not understanding the principles of leadership and
   organization, I backed into a successful project.

3. Dropping Rocks on the Casket —·—·—·—·—·—·— 37
   Scared and fumbling, the mistakes at my first funeral
   became the basis for evangelism.

4. Who Stole the Bride? —·—·—·—·—·—·—·—·—·— 47
   The first wedding I conducted was not a dignified
   event, but included some down-home fun.

5. The Toilet Paper Incident —·—·—·—·—·—·—·— 57
   I had to learn delegation as a young pastor.

6. I Haven't Had Healing 201 Yet! —·—·—·—·—·— 65
   I was not prepared to pray for the sick, so someone
   who needed healing taught me.

7. A Deathbed Conversion —·—·—·—·—·—·—·—·— 75
   I did not know how to approach an atheist, or a person
   facing death, so I followed my heart.

8. Sensationalizing Mr. Sweeney's Son —·—·—·—·— 87
   Everyone thought Mr. Sweeney's son went to hell
   because of the unpardonable sin. I determined to set
   them straight about the issue.

9. Losing the War of the Streetlights —·—·—·—·— 97
   My opposition to the social gospel almost placed me in
   a battle with my people.

10. **"I Saw Jesus"** ————————— 107
How does a preacher respond when one of his leaders claims Jesus visited in his home?

11. **Whose Church Is It Anyway?** ————— 115
My first elders' meeting was a fiasco that made me want to resign.

12. **No One Came to Vacation Bible School** ——— 125
I planned for the greatest Vacation Bible School the church had ever had, but no one came. Failure taught me about advertising.

13. **It Takes Only One** ————————— 135
We experienced atmospheric revival because one person came to pray at the altar.

14. **Ice Cream Paid for My First Car** ———— 143
I was absolutely not going to compromise by raising money with a ladies' bake sale, but I ate the ladies' ice cream.

15. **A Boy's First Love: Gertrude** ————— 151
My first love—Gertrude—came from the ladies of the church.

16. **The Illusion of Dreams That Keep Us Going** —— 155
Because I did not understand leadership, I let my dreams die.

17. **The Coat Thrower** ———————— 163
My love of preaching led to abuses. I had to learn how to correct misdirections.

18. **When the Jar Breaks** ——————— 173
What I thought was the best visual aid to enhance a Sunday School lesson ended in a fiasco.

19. **Becoming Baptist** ————————— 179
Westminster Presbyterian Church entered the Baptist church through the back door; one thousand miles away I entered the Baptist church through the front door.

Epilogue ——————————— 190

Foreword

In 1969, I graduated from Bible college, received my ordination and married. Now it was time to seek my first pastorate, and I was full of anticipation. So I was thrilled when I found out that I was being considered as a candidate by two churches. The first was an established, medium-size church that offered a good salary and had a committed congregation; the other was a tiny church in a small rural community. After praying and talking with my dad (a minister and district superintendent), I decided to take Dad's advice and pursue the small church, where I could learn how to be a pastor "from the ground up."

So my first pastorate was in the small town of Hillham, Indiana. I knew I was headed for a little church, but that still did not prepare me for my first Sunday morning—only three people had arrived when it was time to start, and my wife, Margaret, and I were two of them! We made it through that morning, and as we became acquainted with the wonderful people of the town, the church grew. By the time we left in 1972, more than 200 people attended the church each Sunday, and our record attendance was 301.

You may be wondering how we were able to experience such tremendous growth so quickly. One of the reasons was that in 1970 I read a book that changed my life. It was called *The Ten Largest*

Sunday Schools in America and What Made Them Grow, and the author was Elmer Towns. As I read about pastors from across the country who were on the "cutting edge" of church growth, I was challenged and inspired to learn everything I could about these pastors.

The men in that Sunday School book were my heroes. Elmer Towns was the one who "introduced" these men to me, so I jumped at a chance in 1975 to attend a conference where he was to be the speaker. I traveled from Ohio to Iowa full of anticipation, and the conference was everything I expected. For two days, I simply soaked in Dr. Towns's wisdom and insight.

Before flying back home, I stopped for lunch at a local restaurant. I was eating alone, still trying to process all the great things I had learned at the conference—when who should walk in but Elmer Towns himself. He knew my name, and the fact that I had attended the pastors' conference. Then he said the most exciting words I had heard all week: "Come have lunch with me." So I sat with my hero—although I could not eat a bite of food. As we chatted and became acquainted, I asked him dozens of questions about church leadership, and hung on to every word. He then asked me to fly back home on the same flight with him so we could extend our time together. It was a dream come true.

A year later, I invited Elmer Towns to speak at my first church-growth conference in Ohio. He did more for me than just teach about church growth—he spent time with me by touring my church, dreaming about God's plan, preparing me for the future and stretching my faith. He gave me a vision for the future when he told me, "The greatest churches have yet to be built."

Since then, Elmer Towns and I have become good friends, and we still spend time together. I continue to enjoy his wisdom and insight. He is one of the greatest influences on me and my ability to grow a church. That is why I know you will enjoy "sitting at his feet" as he shares his wisdom in *Stories About My First Church*. The book is full of insight, laughter and practical principles. As you read, I pray that some of Elmer's never-ending passion will ignite a flame in your heart as it did in mine, inspiring you to do great things for God in your church. Remember, great churches have yet to be built!

John Maxwell
Founder
INJOY, Inc.

"Me and my fiancée, Ruth Forbes"

Introduction

Why a 19-Year-Old Pastor?

When I tell my college students in the '90s that I pastored a church at age 19, they look at one another and think, *A dinosaur!* These young men in college look skeptically at one another because they know they could not do it, nor could their friends do it—but I did it.

"How could Dr. Towns be so young and pastor a church?" a college sophomore recently asked my wife.

"My husband has no fear of failure," my wife told him. "He will try anything he believes God wants him to do."

"He knows many things well," she went on to explain, "but he doesn't know what he doesn't know. He could pastor at age 19 because he has such great confidence in his knowledge, but he doesn't know what is on the other side of the wall—he has no idea of what exists in an unknown world."

I jumped into pastoring Westminster Presbyterian Church in Savannah, Georgia, and did not have a clue how to officiate at a wedding or a funeral, or how to conduct myself during a hospital visit. I had no clue about leadership principles or how to employ management techniques, nor did I know how to minister in the hospital room of a man who was expected to die before dawn.

Because I didn't know what I didn't know, I blundered through my mistakes, walked through embarrassing situations, smiled when I didn't know what to do and kept quiet when I didn't know what to say.

Being a 19-year-old pastor is like trying to start the engines of a jet airliner when you don't know where the right switches are located. Planning a whole year's church program is like taxiing the jet onto the runway; still you don't know what you are doing.

I planned Vacation Bible Schools, revivals, Christmas pageants, picnics and I even painted the whole church building in a whole day. I was flying the jet plane without having a clue how to find my way to an airport or successfully land the plane. The fact that I pastored a church for a year and a half, caused it to grow and won many people to Christ who are still in the faith, and are my friends 40 years later, is a demonstration of the grace of God.

I dedicate this book to all the people of Westminster Presbyterian Church in West Savannah who allowed me to improve my preaching skills there as they obeyed the Word spoken to them. They followed my immature leadership as together we tried to saturate a community for Christ. They loved me and told me I was the greatest preacher, when I was barely average. I told them they were the greatest congregation, when they were barely average. We believed each other's exaggerations, and grew better in the warm sun of each other's admiration.

I must recognize my wife, Ruth, whom I was dating through my student pastoring days. We spent many Friday nights typing and mimeographing the church bulletin for the following Sunday.

My thanks to Linda Elliott for typing the manuscript.

May the lessons help young pastors everywhere laugh at themselves and learn to do their jobs better. May the Lord overlook the weaknesses of this book and use it for His glory.

Sincerely yours in Christ,
Elmer L. Towns, Summer 1996

"My mother and Mrs. Miller, one of the five ladies"

1

The Key to My First Pastorate

When I entered Columbia Bible College at age 17, I had a burning desire to serve Jesus Christ. So the first Saturday night at college I went to the Greyhound Bus Station to hand out gospel tracts to people walking or standing nearby. I preached my first sermon on the street corner of Main and Ervay in Columbia, South Carolina, and always worked two or three Christian service assignments because I wanted to serve Jesus Christ.

When I first arrived at Columbia Bible College, I noticed that several upperclassmen preached at churches on Sundays. Most of these male older students were veterans of World War II, and many of them served in small Southern Baptist churches.

God, give me a church where I can preach, became my constant prayer. I remember telling the Lord, *I am too young to be a preacher; but*

Lord, you can do anything. Praying with all the fervency I had in my heart, I asked for a pastorate. I prayed not so much because I wanted to minister to people, or make hospital visits or do any of the other work a pastor does; I just wanted to preach. I had a great burden to stand in front of a congregation and preach the Word of God.

So when I got my first church assignment, it was not unusual that they called me "Preacher." I was not called "reverend," because I was not ordained. I was not called by any of the other ecclesiastical names such as "minister," "pastor," "bishop" or any other nomenclature. To the people at Westminster Presbyterian Church I was simply called "Preacher," and it was appropriate because preaching was my passion. That's what I did the most and that's how I led the church—I led the congregation through my preaching.

Leading Singing at a
Youth for Christ Rally

On a Saturday night in November 1952, I was leading singing at a Youth for Christ rally in Savannah, Georgia. I had come to Savannah for the weekend specifically to thank my Sunday School class for a financial gift they sent to help pay my room and board at Bible college. When I walked into the Youth for Christ meeting, the director, Ralph Godwin, saw me and asked me to lead the singing. I had been the summertime song leader, so I was delighted to help again that evening.

On the platform I was a bundle of energy. I was an arousing song leader, waving my arms the way a windmill moves, cupping my hands to shout encouragement and patting my foot to speed up the tempo when the singing dragged. Some even called me "forceful." This particular Saturday night Youth for Christ rally was no different, and everyone sang enthusiastically.

One of the by-products of being the song leader is sitting on the platform. Sitting on the platform always reinforced the ego of a young preacher who wanted to make a statement; and I was no different from anyone else wanting to make a statement with his life. So I sat on the platform throughout the program.

Being Asked to Preach
After the meeting, I was standing near the pulpit when Mrs. Silla

Hair looked up and caught my attention. Because the platform was much higher than the floor where she was standing, I squatted down to be on eye level with her.

"Will you preach at my church tomorrow?" Mrs. Hair asked straightforwardly.

Because I understood church protocol, I wondered if she had the authority to ask me to preach at her church. I had no question in my mind about who she was. She always brought her car filled with young people from Westminster Presbyterian Church to the Youth for Christ meetings.

"Don't you have to get permission first?" was my respectful request.

"We don't have a pastor anymore," Mrs. Hair answered my probe, then added, "Independent Presbyterian Church closed us down."

A Background of Westminster Presbyterian Church

We all knew that Independent Presbyterian Church had paid the pastor of Westminster Presbyterian Church. It sponsored Westminster Presbyterian Church for many years because the neighborhood had declined, and attendance had also declined.

The original residents in the neighborhood had worked middle-class white-collar jobs, but blue-collar workers started moving into the neighborhood. When the large two-story homes in the neighborhood were vacated by death or a move, the grand old Victorian homes were divided into small apartments. The new poorer group moving into the renovated apartments lived different lifestyles from those they replaced.

Westminster Presbyterian Church practiced traditional Presbyterian liturgy—such as praying an invocation and singing high-church hymns followed by the Amen. They repeated the Apostles' Creed, the Lord's Prayer and read responsively from both the Old Testament and New Testament. The sermons were based on theology, reason and tradition. Westminster had probably declined because few of the lower-class people moving into the community responded to the liturgy. They preferred enthusiastic, informal revivalistic preaching. They liked gospel singing, not quiet meditative hymns, and they wanted an evangelistic service that resembled a camp meeting, not Presbyterian liturgy.

Persistence Worked

As I was kneeling in front of Mrs. Hair, I repeated her words, "They closed Westminster Presbyterian Church down," not understanding why anyone would close a church.

"But we have a key," Mrs. Hair explained, holding up a solitary key on a short chain. "We opened the building for Sunday School."

Mrs. Hair was a short petite-framed woman in her mid thirties and had a "can do" approach to life. She and four other ladies

I began planning what I was going to preach because I was unprepared for this unexpected preaching assignment. I had just started preaching, and did not yet have a sermon barrel of accumulated old messages.

went house-to-house gathering about 25 to 35 children for Sunday School every Sunday. Energetic Silla Hair never accepted no for an answer.

"Come preach to the ladies and children," Mrs. Hair repeated.

Preaching to ladies and children, however, was not an enticing idea. So I gave her an excuse.

"I have to attend my Sunday School class tomorrow morning," I told Mrs. Hair. "They made a payment on my room and board at Bible college so I need to tell them how much I appreciate their gift."

Mrs. Hair stood there nodding her head affirmatively as though she understood what I was saying. I did not know, though, how persistent she could be, so I immediately forgot about the conversation. I met my friends that night and then went home.

The next morning I attended Sunday School at my home church—Eastern Heights Presbyterian Church. I expressed appreciation to the class while standing at the teacher's desk. I explained to them how God had faithfully provided for my needs, and they were a part of God's provision. Then I sat down.

The door behind the classroom opened. Mrs. Silla Hair stuck her head through the door and beckoned with her finger for me to come into the hall. I was dumbfounded. She had been out in the hall listening, and as soon as I finished speaking she stuck her head through the door. This time she did not *ask* me if I would come to preach, she just assumed I would want to preach.

"We have just enough time to drive across town before 11:00 A.M. for preaching," her excited voice communicated haste.

Mrs. Hair drove a blue five-year-old Plymouth, a 1947 four-door sedan. It took about 30 minutes to drive from the east side of Savannah to the west side. Riding along, I began planning what I was going to preach because I was unprepared for this unexpected preaching assignment. I had just started preaching, and did not yet have a sermon barrel of accumulated old messages.

The previous week at Columbia Bible College a chapel speaker who was anointed with the power of God explained that he had not prepared a message, but was simply sharing what God had given him that morning in his private devotions. So I decided to do the same thing.

My First Sermon at Westminster

The first sermon I preached at Westminster Presbyterian Church was based on 1 Timothy 2:1: "That supplications, prayers, intercessions, and giving of thanks, be made for all men." This sermon was probably my poorest because I rambled. I had no compelling focus; I just gave a running commentary. I read one phrase and explained what it meant. Then I read another and continued the process.

The service that morning was not long. I led the singing, primarily choruses for small children and a few gospel songs for the ladies. Then Mrs. Hair passed around the offering plate, which was followed by my short sermon. We were finished by 11:45.

I explained to Mrs. Hair that I had to go back to my mother's home, gather the clean clothes Mother had washed for me and hitchhike back to Columbia Bible College—a distance of about 150 miles. That would take all afternoon and into the evening. If I did not hitch enough rides, I would need to ride the Greyhound Bus back to Columbia.

Agreeing to Preach Sunday Evening

"If you'll stay to preach the evening service," Mrs. Hair proposed, "we'll pay your train fare back to Columbia." She had already checked—the Southern Railway train left at 7:00 P.M. and arrived in Columbia at 11:00 P.M. Like all other Bible colleges, Columbia Bible College had a curfew, and if I did not return by 10:30 P.M. I would be in trouble.

"I'll write you a note," Mrs. Hair said, thinking that would satisfy me.

It irritated me, however, to think I was a preacher who needed a note for being late, whether the note was from my mother or from one of the ladies in the church. I almost refused her offer and could have missed a great experience of pastoring because of pride.

"I'll do it," I nodded my head in appreciation.

The train fare cost about $5 one way and the ladies gave me $10 for the day. A $5 offering for preaching two sermons was the first financial gift I had received for preaching. I would have preached for nothing. Five dollars was like a thousand when Cokes cost a nickel, bus fare was 8 cents and I was paid 20 cents an hour to wash dishes in the college dining room.

Still, the ladies had not asked me to come back the next week, nor to be their regular pastor. I agreed to preach a Sunday night service, but the church did not usually have one and no one in the neighborhood knew I would be preaching that evening. So all of us decided to go door-to-door and invite everyone to the evening service (only 40 to 50 houses were located in the neighborhood). While I was going door-to-door inviting people to a Sunday evening service, Mrs. Hair and the ladies were inviting everyone to come meet the new pastor. The only problem was that I had not been asked to be the pastor.

Witnessing to the Millers

Mrs. Miller, one of the five ladies who helped in the Sunday School, told me to come by her house around 5:30 for supper. Mrs. Miller was a forty-something procrastinating housekeeper who constantly put off everything. As a result, when I walked into her house, I could smell the decay of dust, cooking odor and heavy stale cigarette smoke throughout the house.

The Millers lived in a large single-floor two-bedroom home built personally by Mr. Miller, but he had never finished the house. I walked into the house at the front door and could see every room and closet in the house because only the two-by-four studs were in place. No wallboards, plaster or dividers had been added. The only enclosed room was the bathroom.

Placed everywhere were piles of junk, piles of newspapers, piles of dirty clothes and stacks of dirty dishes. The dining room table was stacked with jars of jelly, ketchup, mustard and all the condiments most people keep in the refrigerator, as well as bags of sugar, salt and boxes of cereal. Although the table was not clean, at least it was convenient to those sitting at the table. They did not have to go to the kitchen to get what was needed; it was right in front of them.

When I arrived, Mr. Miller was asleep on the couch, mouth wide open and snoring. The stench from him and the beer bottles and the body odor told me he was sleeping off a hangover.

"I want you to tell my oldest daughter how to get saved," Mrs. Miller directed as I sat at the dining room table. The oldest daughter had attended Westminster Sunday School when she was a child, but had not gone back since her mother and the other ladies opened up the church building.

"Ye must be born again," I said, opening my Bible to John 3, the story of Jesus and Nicodemus.

In the next 10 or 15 minutes, I slowly explained to her what it meant to be born again; that it was not church membership, baptism or even belief in your head that Jesus had died on the cross.

"You must receive Jesus Christ into your heart to be born again," I admonished.

I shared the gospel across the cluttered dining table. That afternoon I began to experience what many other ministers have felt; I felt the pressure of expectation. A mother wanted her wayward daughter to be converted and she expected me to do it in one conversation. Having a drunk man sleeping behind me and a worldly daughter stonewalling me, I had little confidence as I witnessed.

I talked to the daughter at length about how Jesus Christ could save her, give her new desires and transform her life. All my attention was on the rebellious daughter. I focused in on her, trying to make her understand what it meant to be born again. I zeroed in on her emotions, trying to get her to feel what it felt like to be lost.

When I pressed for a decision, the daughter said, "Not now, maybe later."

A Sunday Evening Surprise

When I left the Millers' house and crossed an open field toward Westminster Presbyterian Church, I still did not know what my sermon would be that evening. Then it came to me: *Preach to everyone what you just preached to the hardened daughter. "Ye must be born again"* (v. 7, *KJV*).

That was the message the congregation needed, so my Sunday evening sermon was set.

I thought my sermon to the Miller daughter was a failure. I really hoped God would work in her heart and that she would be saved; but she put me off. So I also thought the evening sermon was a failure. Little did I know that the drunk man sleeping on the couch behind me was awakened by my voice.

Later Miller would tell me, "I was too embarrassed to get up and say anything." He just pretended to be asleep.

The Holy Spirit intended the message "Ye must be born again" for Mr. Miller. He listened to every word. Immediately after I left the house by the back door, he jumped into action. He quickly took a bath, put on a suit and white shirt—something he had not done for months—and told his wife to get ready.

"We're going to church," Mr. Miller told his wife.

That evening he slipped in at the back door of the church, and sat in the back row. He did not sit with his wife. She sat where she usually sat, on the second pew with her friends. I preached the same sermon he had heard at home, "Ye must be born again."

As I preached, I had no faith that God would reform a drunk, that Mr. Miller could be born again. Nonetheless, I gave a gospel invitation at the end of the sermon for people to come forward as the congregation sang a song. Immediately when the congregation began singing, Miller left the last pew to walk purposefully down the aisle. Without hesitation, not looking to his wife on the right, he headed straight toward me.

"I want to be born again just like you told my daughter," Mr. Miller said.

I motioned for him to kneel at the altar. He was the first of many to kneel at that altar. He began to cry as we knelt. The Presbyterian

Church that had witnessed the formal liturgy of quiet meditation was transformed that evening into an old-fashioned revivalistic preaching center. Miller had come forward to receive Jesus Christ, so I led him to pray at that altar.

My Official Call to Be the "Preacher"

Mr. Miller worked as yard pilot for the Central of Georgia Railway. After the Sunday evening service he took me in his 1951 Ford to the train station, where I boarded the Southern Railway train for Columbia, South Carolina.

Before I got into Miller's car, Silla Hair asked me, "Will you come back and preach next week?" Then she added, "We want you to be our preacher."

The shepherd they [Westminster Presbyterian Church] hired knew less about shepherding than they did. He was basically just a preacher, so that's what they called me, "Preacher."

That was it; that was my call to be the pastor of Westminster Presbyterian Church. Now, obviously, one woman cannot issue a call for a whole church. Remember, though, Westminster Presbyterian Church was not a constituted church. It was just a building. Silla Hair and four other ladies were God's remnant; they were teaching the Word of God to children every Sunday and they needed a shepherd. The shepherd they hired knew less about shepherding than they did. He was basically just a preacher, so that's what they called me, "Preacher."

When I first started preaching at Westminster Presbyterian Church, it was not recognized by the Savannah Presbytery as a constituted church; it was not even a constituted mission work or Sunday School chapel. To them, it was just an empty building in West Savannah. The Savannah Presbytery, however, decided to take me "Under care of Presbytery," which to other denominations is the equivalent of a license for ministry. The license of ministry does not mean a person is ordained. It means the person is approved for theological study because the primary qualifications for ministry have been met. After formal training, the candidate is then ordained, which means being fully approved for ministry.

"The Inquisition" Challenged Me

A couple of months after I started preaching in West Savannah, a long black Buick pulled up in front of the church one Saturday afternoon, and two ordained Presbyterian ministers stepped out of the car. They entered the pastor's study, which I simply called "the office." I was excited about their coming to the church because I wanted to show off what was happening; that is, I was happy until I found out they were the inquisition. They wanted to know why I had reopened this church without authority.

When I sensed their hostility and antagonism, I was scared.

"Why did you do this?" one of the ministers asked.

I did not know what they were going to do—whether they would shut down the building, shut down preaching services or drop me from care of Presbytery. I was in trouble with them and I knew it. So I did what I always have done when I have been in trouble. I just told them what was happening.

I told them how Mrs. Silla Hair had come to the Youth for Christ rally and invited me to preach, and how Mr. Miller had been converted the following evening. I began talking about the men in the community who were being saved. I talked about Allen Dearing, and two or three other drunks—they had all walked the aisle and been saved.

"How many will attend the worship service tomorrow?" one of the ministers asked.

"Only about 70," I answered.

"That's as many as I'll have," the minister's cool hostility turned warm, and the frowns turned to smiles.

The older pastor glowed, saying, "I remember when I had your enthusiasm; it was my first church in seminary, and I remember getting people saved."

The two pastors got back into their Buick, went back to the Savannah Presbytery and recommended that Westminster Presbyterian Church be reconstituted. They reminded me that I could not bury, marry, baptize or serve communion because I was not yet ordained. They exhorted me, however, to assist in those services and learn the ministry by assisting a pastor.

They assigned Rev. Carroll Stegall as my senior supervisor; he pastored my home church of Eastern Heights Presbyterian Church. I was instructed to call him for baptisms, communion, funerals and weddings. Interestingly enough, in my first year at Westminster Presbyterian Church we baptized by sprinkling more adults into our church than did all the other churches in the Savannah Presbytery. This is not a put-down of them, only an indication that God was beginning to do a work in West Savannah and others began to recognize it.

PRINCIPLES TO TAKE AWAY

1   *The principle of the undeniable call of God to ministry.* The call of God is a deep burden that you must preach the gospel and an exciting compulsion that makes you want to preach the gospel. The call of God involves fruit, for when a "called minister" preaches, God will work through him for the conversion of sinners and growth of His believers. My ministry at Westminster Presbyterian Church reconfirmed to me the call of God into full-time Christian service.

2. *The principle of the larger church.* Although I believe in the sanctity of the duly constituted local church—based on New Testament criteria—I also recognize the "larger" church, which involves missions such as the five ladies were operating at Westminster Presbyterian Church. Their endeavors were blessed of God and the Presbytery recognized the work of God so that they reconstituted it into a local church.

3. *The principle of fruit for faithful service.* Five ladies invited me to come and minister in the community known as West

Savannah. For their faithfulness, the husbands of these ladies either came to know Jesus Christ (two of them hopeless drunks), or they repented of backsliding and became active in local church work.

4. *The principle of the bucket from the well.* The old adage is surely true, "What's in the well, comes up in the bucket." When I did not know what to preach and had not prepared, I simply shared the message from the Scriptures God had put upon my heart. God used the simple messages I preached. People were saved and Mr. Miller was transformed into a dedicated worker for God.

"Westminster Presbyterian Church"

2

Painting the Whole
Church in a Whole Day

Westminster Presbyterian Church was a beautiful old colonial building located in a neighborhood that had once been the home of wealthy middle-class Savannahians. It was approximately two miles from downtown; therefore it was a short carriage ride in the days of the horse and buggy, and later the trolley car that ran down the Old Augusta Road.

The neighborhood was filled with several large Victorian two-story homes built about 1900, around the turn of the century. Each frame house was painted white, and both the first and second levels were graced with large spacious porches designed for evening sitting after a long hot day.

The people of West Savannah had built a colonial sanctuary that extended their lifestyle into the house of God, which also reflected their love of God. The large wood-frame church building had four tall pillars reaching two stories from the front porch to hold up the roof, over which a towering steeple and bell tower pointed toward heaven. The large old bell had been taken out of a steam locomotive, and was a gift of the Central of Georgia Railway to the church.

Many residents in the neighborhood were engineers or conductors working for one of the several railway lines that passed immediately to the south of the neighborhood—Central of Georgia, Savannah and Atlanta Railway, Seaboard Coastline, Atlanta Coastline Railway and Southern Railway.

Originally, Westminster Presbyterian Church consisted of a large auditorium seating approximately 400, and seven vaulted windows were placed on either side—each arch told people this was a sacred building. Some of the windows were stained glass, others were just smoked Depression glass designed in small sections divided by leaded strips.

In time, however, the large auditorium was divided into five Sunday School rooms, bathrooms, a pastor's study and the smaller sanctuary that seated 175.

Presenting the Painting Idea

The building is one big paint blister, I observed soon after I became pastor of Westminster Presbyterian Church. It was years since the building had been painted, so the white paint was cracked, puckered and chalky. I could see raw wood between the gaping cracks in the paint and the weather-beaten siding was beginning to rot. I noticed crumbling window frames, broken molding and loose deck board on the front porch.

"Your church doesn't need revival," a resident told me when I was trying to present Christ to him, "your church needs a coat of paint."

I was embarrassed. Whether the man was right or not, he influenced my thinking. As I looked at the sagging framing and decaying building, I decided if we painted it visitors might come to church. I really thought that painting the building would attract the area's residents to the church. Naively, I thought they would come to a clean repainted building.

Later, I learned people don't visit because of facilities, but because of excitement and the power of the gospel. What I did not realize was that community involvement in painting the old building would attract many of them to Christ. When the members took pride in their church building, their renewed loyalty produced excitement, which caused the rest of the community to visit and see what was happening.

As a young preacher, I was deeply into presenting object lessons. So the Sunday following my observations about the needed paint job, without any planning, any committees or much forethought, I announced to the small congregation, "See this piece of blue chalk?"

I held up the blue chalk to tell them that blue chalk could make a difference in the church.

"God could bring revival to the church through this blue chalk," I told the congregation.

They [the congregation] had all grasped the idea of "painting the whole church in a whole day." They quickly made the idea their idea.

I explained that the same week on Saturday morning I was going to start at the front porch and walk around the building, drawing a blue line every 10 feet. I dramatically pretended to draw a blue line from high in the sky down to the floor.

Then using all the authority of an army sergeant telling young recruits what to do, I announced, "I am going to write your name on your 10 feet."

I explained that each family name would be written in blue chalk on the bottom of one particular section. Each family group would have to start painting under the eaves and paint down to the lowest board, finally painting over their name.

"We can paint the whole church in a whole day," I challenged.

The Idea Became Their Idea

Like a sky filled with lightning during a summer storm, the small audience bristled with electricity. For the next two or three minutes

I continued to explain the project, but no one listened to me. People began whispering to one another. At the time, I was not sure if they were rebelling or supporting my idea.

Mr. Seckinger raised his hand, which was the custom in this small church at announcement time.

"I got a two-story extension ladder, we're going to need a lot more than one ladder," the old man explained.

He told the audience that we would need a lot of extension ladders if everyone was going to paint at the same time. I had not thought about the ladders.

Then going on, he mentioned, "I am too old to get up on a ladder, but I'll get my son to do my section."

"We gotta have a lot of tall ladders," another one of the men said. "I'll start rounding them up from the neighborhood."

"We need to get the ladies organized for a picnic dinner," the Mrs. Smith in charge of Ladies Auxiliary said. (Three Mrs. Smiths attended the church.)

"Who's going to get the paint?" Mr. Strickland asked.

He was a plumbing contractor and understood what it meant to buy supplies for workers. I had not thought about the paint.

"I'll get the paint, and the brushes and the thinner. There will be a lot of things to get ready before Saturday," the plumbing contractor announced. I had not thought about any of the supplies.

The people were all jabbering among themselves. The idea was captivating. They had all grasped the idea of "painting the whole church in a whole day." They quickly made the idea their idea. The buzz of whispered conversation was not disrespectful, nor was it rebellious. It was like pouring milk into Rice Krispies and listening to snap, crackle and pop. They all had ideas, and they were all telling someone else what they thought.

I learned that morning that ideas are powerful tools for leaders to move a congregation. The idea of "painting the whole church in a whole day" was much greater than the sermon I preached that day. I don't remember what I preached, and I doubt anyone paid much attention.

At the end of the sermon, I stood at the back door to "shake them out"; they all told me what they were going to do about painting the church. Some ladies talked about bringing lunch, others talked about what needed to be done and others told me exactly what they wanted to paint.

Painting Day Arrived

That next week at Columbia Bible College, I did not think much about the project. I only remembered to pray, "God, help us to paint the whole church in a day, so people will want to attend church." Then I added, "And please may no one get hurt falling off a ladder."

Usually, Friday nights were date nights for Ruth and me; but that week I arranged to travel home on Friday afternoon because I wanted to be there early Saturday morning. I had told everyone we would begin at 7:00 A.M., before the heat of the noon. It was just too hot to ask laypeople to stand in the blistering sun during the noonday to paint a gleaming white building.

Saturday morning, I rode up to the church on my bicycle at about 10 minutes to 7; the place was already a beehive of activity. Already the church was surrounded by cars and pickup trucks, and a paint contractor's truck was backed up on the sidewalk to the front porch.

Although not a member of the church, a contractor who attended a Baptist church said, "It's too dangerous for someone to try to paint the ceiling of the porch; it's two-stories tall." He constructed his scaffolding and did the dangerous work in two hours.

When I arrived, at least a dozen long ladders were leaning up against the cracking paint of the building. On the front porch were placed dozens of gallons of white Old Dutchboy paint—Mr. Strickland had received a donation from a local paint distributor. Blankets spread everywhere on the lawn were covered with babies, diaper bags and teenage girls intermittently playing and changing diapers.

I sent a couple of the junior boys scurrying through the church and around the building to gather everyone to the front porch for prayer. People had come whom I had never seen in my life, and would probably never see again; they had come to help us paint the church. They were captivated by the idea of "Painting the whole church in a whole day."

Many forces were at work that day that I did not understand: community pride, and helping friends who were members of the church. Several fathers helped paint just because their children attended our Sunday School.

"Let's get with it," one middle-aged father yelled. "I still want to get some fishing in today."

Asking God's Blessing on the Project

"We need to pray first," I announced from the front porch to the crowd standing on the grass, and then lifting my hand as if in pastoral benediction, I prayed, "Lord, this is Your house, bless the efforts we do for this house, that they may be for Thee."

I not only prayed to God for His blessing, but I was also "semi-preaching" in my prayers to make sure everyone understood why we were painting the building. "Help that no one would fall from a ladder, mixes the paint wrongly, or spills paint on anyone else."

"Start the marking!" someone yelled immediately, "we're burning sunlight"—a Southern expression that means we should not waste time.

I was serious in my prayer, but I remember hearing several snickers throughout the crowd when I prayed that people might not get spattered with paint. Of course, I prayed, "Help every unsaved person here today to find Jesus as Savior, and may this building be a lighthouse for hundreds of children to come and find Him as their Savior. Amen."

"We're Burning Sunlight"

"Start the marking!" someone yelled immediately, "we're burning sunlight"—a Southern expression that means we should not waste time.

Holding the blue chalk in my hand, I began marking at the left of the front door and worked down the front porch to my right. After stepping off 10 paces, I wrote the name "MILLER" in caps, indicating that the Miller family would paint this first section, including the stained-glass window. After 10 more steps I wrote the name "HAIR," for Silla Hair who had been instrumental in persisting that I be the preacher of the church.

As I continued marking the steps around the church, several people volunteered for different sections of the building, some wanting to paint around the window of their classrooms, others wanting to paint around a particular stained-glass window. Almost immediately after I drew the blue line, a ladder was thrown up against the building, and squeaks could be heard as someone climbed to the top. Then systematically the noise began—*Scrrr...scrrr.*

The scraping began and the powdered paint puffed out into the morning breeze like dust rising off a dry country road. Those below were peppered with falling paint particles as the scraping began—*Scrrr...scrrr...scrrr...*

When I came to the section behind the pulpit, I said I wanted to paint it because the pulpit was mine. Mr. Strickland disagreed.

"No, we need you to walk around and inspire everybody," he explained. Then he suggested, "Get a paint brush and bucket and paint a little in everybody's section. That'll make everybody happy, and nobody will give up."

I thought it was a good idea, so I assigned the back of the pulpit to someone else and kept marking off 10-foot sections until we had completely circled the church. As though God in His sovereignty looked down from heaven to bless the endeavor, the exact number of families were present to equal the exact number of sections I had stepped off around the church.

Like a swarm of ants scurrying over an ant hill, the people of West Savannah scurried over the outside walls of Westminster Presbyterian Church with enthusiasm and pride, the likes of which I have not seen in any church in my life.

I heard yelling, talking, laughing and teasing from one group of workers to another. After about 45 minutes, someone broke into song—an old-fashioned gospel hymn. To this day I don't remember what they sang, but it was uplifting to hear people who were surrounding the church building with paint surrounding the building with their voices. They sang the old songs that church people and nonchurch people knew, and everyone joined in.

I went from section to section painting a little bit on every section. Wanting to make some kind of contribution, I chose to paint the bottom two boards on the church, all the way around the church. In doing so, I was the one who covered up all the names.

Mr. Strickland instructed two men to rip out the rotting boards and replace them with new lumber. The sound of a power saw could be heard a block in each direction, telling the whole neighborhood that life and pride were being practiced at Westminster Presbyterian Church.

At about 9:30 A.M., the Baptist paint contractor finished the ceiling of the front porch, then folded up his scaffold, packed it on top of the truck and left.

Ripping Out the Carpet

I was standing inside the front hallway with Mr. Strickland, and the musty smell of the corridor was a stark contrast to the crisp clean smell of paint outside the building.

"We need to freshen up the inside, just like the outside," Strickland said to me.

"It really stinks in here; it smells like old people, or it smells nasty like poor people's houses who never clean," he went on to make his point.

This was an answer to prayer. I was embarrassed by the stale smell in the church building and had prayed for God to take it away. Although I had asked God to take away the smell inside the building, God did not answer that prayer the way I expected. The amazing way God would answer this prayer taught me something about Him. When we ask God to do something, He sometimes puts the ball back into our courts and shows us how to get the job done.

"It's this rug that stinks up the whole church house," Strickland said to me. Then the two of us got down on our hands and knees, put our noses down to the rug and crawled along smelling the old rotten, worn rug. It was probably 40 years old.

"Let's see what's under it," Strickland said to me. He went over to the corner of the hallway, took a hammer and ripped the rug up at the corner. "There's a hardwood floor underneath, a beautiful maple hardwood," he discovered.

The yellowing tarnished hardwood flooring badly needed painting. Sand in the rug had worked its way between the floor and the mat, grinding the paint off the hardwood floor. Although it needed paint, it did not look as bad as did the worn-out rug, and it certainly would not smell.

"Do you think you and I could rip this carpet out of here before any of the elders saw us?" Strickland asked me. He was going to do something I later would learn as a principle in leadership: It is easier to receive forgiveness than it is to receive permission.

"Sure."

"Let's do it."

Down the hall we started ripping off the rug. I pulled the rug,

Strickland was on his hands and knees, prying out the carpet tacks.

"Don't take it outside," he warned me, "somebody will see it." Then he went on to explain, "We don't want the women to know what we're doing yet."

Twelve long pews lined each side of the auditorium. It was easy to unscrew the floor bolts and slip a pew across the aisle between the pews on the other side for temporary storage until we lifted up the carpet on one side. Within 30 minutes, the carpet in half the auditorium was ripped up and pulled to the center. Within another 30 minutes, the rest of the auditorium carpet had been pulled to the center and rolled into the center aisle. We did not remove the carpet on the platform because it was inlaid under the base molding. It also would have taken too long to remove the carpet and replace the molding.

When we had all the carpet unloosed and ready to move, we called several of the men to help us. Out the double doors we pulled, grunted and shoved the massive carpet out onto the street, not knowing what the ladies would say.

Of course, once the ladies discovered what we had done, they had to go inside and inspect the floor. They all agreed that we needed to get rid of the carpet. Later, I had to admit the preaching in the auditorium sounded better without that absorbent wool rug soaking up every word. The singing also sounded better than it ever had before. The next day our voices bounced off the floor and reverberated off the walls and ceiling.

"Put It On Thick"

By 12 noon on that Saturday morning, most of the painting was done. Those who finished early helped those who did not have as many family members. Because we had started at the top and painted down, an early-morning picture of the church building looked as though it were under siege, dozens of people on ladders trying to conquer the church building at the same time. By noon, however, the white building glistened in the noonday sun. When looking closely at the boards, though, it was obvious that the church needed a second coat of paint. The original coat had been so weather-beaten and faded in comparison to the glistening white new coat of paint that no one seemed to care. No one offered to come back next week to paint a second coat.

"Put it on thick," Strickland kept saying as he walked around the church supervising what people were doing. He had sent some people back up the ladder to paint a thicker coat before the first coat was dry, just because he could see the grain of wood through the paint.

Experiencing *Koinonia*

A church congregation experiences great satisfaction in sitting on the front lawn, eating fried chicken, potato salad and homemade buttermilk biscuits, then gazing admiringly at a freshly painted building each one just helped create. I sat among the people, my knees crossed, chewing on about my fifth leg of chicken. I felt like a conquering general who had just won a great battle, or a student finishing an exam in which he knew he had earned an *A*. To feel the friendship of dozens of church members and their friends and neighbors, all sitting around talking, is one of the greatest experiences any pastor can have. It was *koinonia*—what the Bible describes as "fellowship one with another."

By the time we finished "painting the whole church in a whole day," I had turned from age 19 to 20; and even that tender age was too young to pastor a church. What my age could not do for me, or mitigate against me, however, was overcome that day.

PRINCIPLES TO TAKE AWAY

1. *The principle of the power of credible vision.* I did not understand leadership principles or how to assign tasks to people, I just led them. When I challenged them to "paint the whole church in a whole day," I learned the power a leader can have in motivating people to serve the Lord. All I had to do was to give them a task, a believable task, an achievable task and a task they wanted to do. This task was simply a vision that we could "paint the whole church in a whole day."

2. *The principle of on-site credibility.* The people "bought into" my challenge to "paint the whole church in a whole day" because I was part of the vision. I walked around the church to paint a part of every person's section and stayed

with them from beginning to end. That day I learned it is not how much I do; it is how much I can get others to do.

3. *The principle of vision before details.* What I did not understand at the time about leadership, I know now. We lead through vision. When I exhibited the leadership role, I gave the people a vision of painting the whole church first before I plunged into the details of paint, ladders, brushes and the hundreds of other details it would take to "paint the whole church in a whole day." When the vision was adequately sold to the people, however, and they bought into the vision, there was enough power in that vision to attract people alongside to get the job done. They took care of all the details. I have learned as a leader that if I can get the people excited about a task, they will make it work.

4. *The principle of questionable decisions.* Mr. Strickland and I ripped out carpet that had been on the floor for probably 40 years. Whether we should was not the question; we did it and were willing to take the consequences. Too often leaders won't take responsibility for their ideas. They run to get permission from others because they avoid accountability; but Mr. Strickland and I saw a problem, saw what was the right thing to do and we did it.

"'Ashes to ashes...' became a huge embarrassment"

3

Dropping Rocks on the Casket

"I've never preached at a funeral!" I told my mother when I walked into the house at 107 Wagner Street in Savannah, Georgia. I was still 19 years old and had never had a course in pastoral theology. I did not even know there was such a book as the *Star Ministerial Manual*, which explained exactly what a pastor should say and pray at a funeral. As far as I knew, I was just supposed to stand in front of the people to preach and pray what God put upon my heart.

I had arrived home around one o'clock on Saturday afternoon. Early that morning at six I left Columbia, South Carolina, on the Southern Railway train. In Savannah I transferred to a city bus, transferring twice, each time barely making my connection.

That was the quickest connection I ever got across Savannah, I thought as I walked into my mother's house. I did not realize that God in His sovereignty had worked out the quick connection so I could preach the funeral sermon of an 82-year-old member of my church who had died two days earlier. They told my mother to get me to the church as quickly as possible.

"They're waiting at the church for you," my mother told me as I came into the house. To my shocked response, she told me, "Hurry as fast as you've ever gone."

I quickly put on a white shirt, tie and black suit. At 19 years of age, it was important to impress people in how I dressed because it

---

At that funeral, I would suffer one of my most humiliating moments as a pastor; but then in defeat and humiliation God would use me more in my brokenness than for any other single experience at Westminster Presbyterian Church.

---

made me look more mature. I rolled up my pant leg, stuck my Bible under my belt buckle, jumped on my racing bike and scooted down Wheaton Street, heading seven miles across town to Westminster Presbyterian Church.

I was speeding and I knew I could make the run across town in 35 minutes. I prayed for the Lord to help every light be green so I could just whiz through, and He answered my prayer.

What am I going to say? I thought all the way to the church. I pedaled as fast as I could, not wanting to be late; yet I did not want to get there at all. I was on the spot; I had to preach a sermon and I did not have a clue what to do.

People seemed to expect a lot from a 19-year-old preacher, simply because he had preached sermons that helped people be born again.

Little did I know what would happen at that funeral. I would suffer one of my most humiliating moments as a pastor; but then in defeat and humiliation God would use me more in my brokenness than for any other single experience at Westminster Presbyterian Church.

Officiating at My First Funeral

Instructions from My Mentor

As I ran in at the back door of the church, I was met by Rev. Carroll Stegall, senior pastor of Eastern Heights Presbyterian Church. The Savannah Presbytery had assigned him to supervise me. No one could miss him; he was a large man who always wore a bow tie and a light-colored suit. His salt and pepper or graying hair revealed his advancing age. He had retired as a foreign missionary from the Belgian Congo and came home to pastor the church in which I grew up.

Looking at me through small, rimless, wire spectacles—the kind Harry Truman wore—Stegall said with a knowing smile, "I heard you had your first funeral and I thought you wouldn't know what to do, so I've come to help you."

Ain't God good, I thought in crude English, but expressed a hallelujah to God for answers to prayer. I was grateful for Stegall's presence because I did not know what to do at the funeral.

"Let's go over the order of service," Stegall said, motioning us to go to my study. "You can talk to the family after we get the program arranged."

By now it was a few minutes before 2:00 P.M. and I suddenly felt secure. Having the help of Rev. Carroll Stegall, this funeral would be done the proper way.

"Where is your ministerial manual?" Stegall asked me.

"What's that?" was my abrupt question.

He laughed and shook his head with a smile.

"Just do what I tell you to do," and receiving that instruction I walked out to officiate at my first funeral.

The Seal of God's Spirit Was on His Heart

George Kessler, the 82-year-old deceased man, was the father of Silla Hair, one of the women instrumental in pursuing me to be the pastor of Westminster Presbyterian Church. I had been in her home the previous Sunday evening after the evening service, and in chatting with Mr. Kessler, I asked the same question I had asked of everyone else, "Have you been born again?"

"I sure have," the feeble man told me without hesitation. He nodded his head, approving of my question and said, "I have the seal of God's Spirit in my heart."

He told me he was of German descent and had come from the Salsburger community approximately 35 miles in the direction we call "up in the country." The community was located up the Savannah River where the Salsburgers first settled when they came to Georgia with John Wesley. He told me that as a boy he had met Jesus Christ and had been born again. I believed the man, and after I left the home I did not think about Mrs. Hair's aging father again until I was told he had passed away.

Following the Leader's Lead

The funeral went well. I stood and read the Scriptures when Rev. Stegall called on me, and then later I stood and led in prayer when he called on me.

"We'll walk in front of the casket out the door," he whispered to me. "You follow my lead, the funeral director will roll the casket out behind us."

The internment of the body to the grave was to take place in the old Salsburger cemetery approximately 35 miles away. Rev. Stegall did not have time to make the long trip into the country and to return that afternoon, so he gave me careful instructions about what to do. As he instructed me, my stomach began to tighten again. He was not going with me.

"When you first get there, stand at the rear of the hearse," Stegall said.

Stegall told me I should wait there until the family arrived. Then he explained that when the pallbearers took the casket out of the hearse I should lead the family to the open grave and stand at the head (i.e., where the head of the body would be placed).

This seemed simple to me. Then Stegall told me I was to wait until the family was seated, then gather all the friends to stand around.

He told me to read John 14:1-3, offer a prayer and commit the man's body to the grave, and then offer condolences to each member of the family seated in the first row. After that I was to go and stand out of the way and the funeral director would be responsible for dismissing the mourners.

"That's it?"

"That's it."

"Sounds easy to me," I said.

The funeral procession then proceeded toward the Salsburger

cemetery, and I rode in the front seat of the hearse for 35 miles.

Thus far, everything went well. I waited at the rear of the hearse; the pallbearers picked up the casket and I led them to our assigned place. After the family was seated, I did as I was instructed. I read Scripture, but rather than reading it, I quoted it from memory.

I said, "Ashes to ashes, dust to dust,"

and squeezed the hardened clay,

but it did not turn to sand in my hand.

Ashes to Ashes, Dust to Dust

Then my problem began. In some movies I had seen the pastor pick up dirt and spread it onto the casket, saying, "Ashes to ashes, dust to dust."

So before I prayed, I picked up some red Georgia clay. The only trouble was that it was not porous sand that could fall between your fingers. I picked up a large clod of hardened red Georgia clay. It had been dug out of the deep wet earth, but now in the blazing sun had turned brick hard. I held my hand out over the gaping hole and said, "Ashes to ashes, dust to dust," and squeezed the hardened clay, but it did not turn to sand in my hand.

I was flustered and my ears turned red.

Twisting the clay in my hand to get a better grip, I even tried to break it in half with my thumb; I squeezed again as hard as I could. Everyone saw what I was doing. My embarrassment deepened. I silently prayed, *Dear Lord, help me break this clod; I am embarrassed.*

Then clearing my throat, I began again, "Ashes to ashes, dust to dust."

Then mustering up the last ounce of energy in my body, I squeezed as hard as possible and shook my fist to break the clod, but to no avail. I had three clods in my hand and I tried to rub them together to break them, but that did not help. Then, as a boy who is learning to break two pecans together in one hand, I tried to break the clods one against the other; but nothing happened. In desperation, I held my hand over the gaping hole and dropped the hardened clods of clay onto the casket.

Thwang. The first clod hit the top of the metal top of the casket, its sheet metal lid echoing like small stones thrown onto a tin roof.

Thwang! As the second clod hit the casket top, I closed my eyes in embarrassment.

Thwang. The third clod echoed a finality.

I felt every eye of the family and friends staring at me. I was hotter with embarrassment than the heat of the Georgia sun that hung like a red wafer in the sky.

"Let us pray," I announced. "Lord, help us."

I do not know if my request was more for my embarrassment, or for the grieving family about the loss of an 82-year-old father and grandfather. I stumbled through the prayer.

Then I went and shook hands with each family member and offered my condolences. I told each one that we would see the deceased again in the resurrection.

Encouraging Words: "They Like You"

As soon as possible, I escaped the crowd to stand by the hearse. I wanted the protection of the front seat so no one could see me, or better, laugh at me. It was one of those moments when I wanted to be by myself. I did not want to talk to the funeral director who walked over to me when he had finished helping the family into the limousine. He held out a daisy in his hand, and waited for me to receive it.

As I reached out my open hand, he dropped the daisy into my palm and said, "Squeeze this flower."

I tightened my fist around the daisy, but did not squeeze it as tight as he suggested.

"Go ahead, squeeze it; it'll crush in your hand; it is not hard Georgia clay. Next time use a flower, not red Georgian clay."

I squeezed the daisy and let the petals fall to the ground. That small act was therapy. It was a relief to see the white petals fall toward the weeds of the cemetery grounds.

The funeral director explained that he saw what had happened. He told me not to be embarrassed, that all the family and friends were pulling for me.

Then he said some very encouraging words: "They like you; you'll be all right."

I said nothing as the hearse drove 35 miles back to the church. When they dropped me off at the church on the corner of Fourth and Alexander Street, one of the pallbearers invited me, "Come on down to Silla Hair's house and get something to eat."

Southern Hospitality

In the South, friends and families bring food for the loved ones at a funeral. The kitchen is stacked with food, much like a church potluck dinner. Everything is there, from fried chicken to snap beans to biscuits to corn bread and yeast dinner rolls. Mrs. Hair's kitchen table was as packed as any church supper I have ever seen.

We filled our plates and I went back into the dining room where 24 chairs circled the edge of the room. The dining room table had been removed; the deceased's body had been kept in the coffin in this room for viewing before the funeral. Now the room was empty except for a circle of people who all sat around eating, not knowing what to say to one another.

The Season of the Soul
When people had finished eating, there was a moment of silence. No one knew what to say. Silla Hair, daughter of the deceased, turned to me and beckoned, "Preacher, what do you have to say to us?"

I honestly did not know what to say. I had never been in this kind of a situation before; but I always knew how to present Jesus Christ, and to ask the people if they had been born again. I turned in my Bible to John 3 and read the story of Nicodemus who had came to Jesus by night.

Jesus told him, "Except a man be born again, he cannot see the kingdom of God" (v. 3, *KJV*). Jesus went on to tell Nicodemus that being born again was not of flesh, nor of water, but a person had to be born again by the Holy Spirit.

Late that afternoon as the sun was setting and an early evening was approaching, I preached a 20-minute sermon to that family sitting in a circle around the dining room. I preached, "Ye must be born again."

It was the same sermon I had preached at the Millers' house in West Savannah prior to Mr. Miller's being saved. Here was another opportunity to witness to people I would not see again; people who came from many areas and were gathered in a moment of grief. I preached the new birth. When I finished my sermon, I started around the room asking each one individually the same question.

"Have you been born again?"

Almost all of them told me yes; or they simply nodded their heads in approval. I think they answered as they thought they should. I did not think all of them were born again, but I did not confront them. I simply let each person respond as he or she wanted.

The Results of Planted Seed

During the next year, many of those who had sat in that room came to the church to listen to me preach, and at the gospel invitation walked forward to receive Jesus Christ as Savior. In almost every instance, they began thinking about being saved in Silla Hair's dining room after the funeral. They reminded me that I had put them on the spot when I asked the question, "Have you been born again?"

They reminded me that the question penetrated deeply, perhaps because they were thinking about death; the question was more meaningful than at any other time in their lives.

Silla Hair had been married three times. Because of the funeral and my sermon in her dining room, two of her former husbands were saved—Allen and Ernest.

Today, I look back at the funeral and chuckle at my naiveté and brashness. I wanted to do the right thing in the right way. I wanted to make a good impression; yet people in the community chuckled for several years, remarking that I was the pastor who "dropped rocks on the casket."

PRINCIPLES TO TAKE AWAY

1. *The principle of anointed brokenness.* Sometimes God cannot use us because of our pride or arrogance; we simply will not let go of our egos and allow God to work through us. So God must break us, sometimes embarrassing us with the things we hold dearest, such as preaching a funeral or preparing to pray.

2. *The principle of planted seed.* That day I planted the seed of

the gospel in the hearts of many people, but, of course, they had heard the message before. The difference was that at their moment of brokenness (i.e., the death of a loved one) they were more receptive to the message of salvation than they were at any other time in their lives. I did something they had never experienced before—I put them on the spot. I asked them if they had been born again.

3. *The principle of receptivity.* I have often preached the gospel to people who are not ready for it, but sometimes questions such as "Have you been born again?" prepare their hearts for a time when they will later receive Christ as Savior. So God taught me to look for moments of receptivity in the hearts of the people and use His Word to make them responsive to the message.

4. *The principle of the "season of the soul."* Timing controls everything in life, even the timing of when people come to know Jesus Christ as Savior. There is a time to be born, a time to be saved and a time to die. Little did I know when I walked into the dining room of a bereaved family that it was their "season of the soul" when they were open to being converted. I preached the gospel and they responded, not immediately, but later.

"Officiating at an unusual wedding"

4

Who Stole the Bride?

Every preacher wants his first wedding to be proper. Mine ended in a fiasco of gigantic proportions. When I say gigantic proportions, I could be talking about the bride, or I could be talking about the incidents of the evening or I could be talking about what I thought would be repercussions throughout the whole community.

Meet the Bride and Groom

Edith had grown up in the community, and throughout her childhood had attended both Vacation Bible School and Sunday School; however, not regularly since her teen years. I wish I could say that Ernest also grew up in the church community, but he didn't.

Edith met Ernest in a bar, and when I found out about it, I was speechless. I was presenting the usual premarriage counseling sessions to Edith and Ernest when I casually asked, "Where did you two meet?"

"The Evergreen Bar," Ernest answered with straightforward honesty.

Because Ernest had not been around my kind of preacher, he did not know what I thought about drinking, or my view of separation from sin.

God had blessed the first marriage, and because all institutions are in fact instituted by God, marriage whether between believers or unbelievers should have God's blessing.

Then to compound the problem, Ernest went on to add, "The Evergreen Bar is not hard to find," his drawl slowly dropped his words in front of me. "It's the one by the Evergreen Motel; you know, that's the cheap motel with those little cabins out back."

I was flustered. My pure mind immediately rushed to evil thoughts—perhaps Edith went to this bar to pick up a man, she met Ernest and they went straight to one of the little cabins to commit fornication.

I wanted to stop the counseling session right there. I wanted to say that I would not be a part of an unholy alliance, or any other sins of the flesh. The wisest thing I ever did, however, was not to blurt out what was on my mind. The wisest thing I did was to let them talk. So I let them tell the whole story.

May I quickly add that my view of marriage as a young preacher was not as broadminded as it should have been. I thought that marriage was meant only for the sanctified, and that God ultimately blessed those marriages in which a man and woman met each other in virginal purity, and the wedding night was the first time they made love. My holy view of marriage was surpassed only by my holy desire to return this sacred institution to its original loftiness.

I did not understand that marriage was an institution—the inevitable union of a man and woman ordained by God, blessed by the Church and legally constituted by the State. God had blessed the first marriage, and because all institutions are in fact instituted by God, marriage whether between believers or unbelievers should have God's blessing. Edith and Ernest were doing the right thing.

Ernest continued to talk about the Evergreen Bar, how he saw Edith in a booth with her two friends, then he went over to her and asked her to dance and she accepted.

Again, I interrupt the narrative to remind you that as a young minister I preached against dancing. I told people it was another tool of Satan to corrupt youth. Ernest, however, did not know my perspective at the time. He had not heard my preaching. Displaying the naiveté of a six-year-old driving a car, Ernest continued to relate all the events of how he met Edith. Obviously, he did not see the disapproval on my face as he continued to expound event upon event upon event.

I decided not to confront the events or the Evergreen Bar or Motel. I decided just to present the principles of God's Word and let the Holy Spirit apply them to Ernest's life. I am sure the Holy Spirit spoke to Ernest's heart; but I am not sure he understood everything I said. I explained the whole marriage outline provided in the ministerial manual, indicating the role of a husband in a Christian home, and the role of the wife in that home.

Arranging the Wedding

Two or three things had to occur before the couple could proceed with the wedding. First, I was not an ordained Presbyterian minister; I was only licensed by the Savannah Presbytery. Therefore I was not legally qualified to tie the knot. So I contacted the appointed counselor by the Presbytery, Rev. Carroll Stegall, and he agreed to conduct the official part of the ceremony.

As I was talking to him on the phone, he asked, "When is the rehearsal?"

"What's a rehearsal?" I asked.

Rev. Stegall stuttered over the next sentence, then chuckled. When his end of the phone became quiet, I knew I was in trouble.

He slowly explained to me why a rehearsal had to be planned before weddings, just so everyone knew what to do.

"This family doesn't want a rehearsal," I explained to my senior counselor. "She comes from a poor family, and the flowers will come out of her garden."

Then I explained that the bride would not wear a wedding dress, but the couple was getting married in "Sunday go-to-meeting clothes." They had explained they did not have enough money for all the fixin's and trimmin's.

"We'll meet 30 minutes before the wedding, and I will go over the service with you," Rev. Stegall told me.

The wedding was arranged for a Saturday night, so I arrived in Savannah, Georgia, Saturday morning from Columbia Bible College. That day I did my usual visitation in the homes and hospitals. When I arrived at the church, I saw that Edith's family was preparing for the wedding.

Two or three bushes were planted in buckets and arranged where the pulpit usually was located. The pulpit was moved to the side of the platform. The communion table was also moved to the side; dozens of plants in clay pots had been placed where the communion table had previously been standing. Although not as beautiful as a florist might arrange, in its simplicity it was an appropriate altar for a wedding ceremony.

The bride's mother was preparing for the reception in the Sunday School assembly area. She had brought a large punch bowl containing punch, a home-baked cake and several plates of cookies. Although it was simple, it was adequate for the evening.

When Rev. Stegall arrived, we looked through the ministerial manual and I marked off those sections in the service for which I was responsible.

Conducting a Simple Ceremony

The ceremony was quick and simple. When it came to the technical pronouncement, Rev. Stegall said, "By the authority of the Westminster Presbyterian Church, and the state of Georgia, I pronounce you husband and wife."

I read Scripture and closed in prayer.

Immediately after the service, Rev. Stegall and I took the couple into my office. There we signed the marriage license and gave the document to the groom.

"Who do I pay?" Ernest looked at me inquiringly.

I had never faced such a question in my life. I had absolutely no idea that people paid the preacher at a wedding. I just assumed it was a part of pastoral duties.

Turning to Rev. Stegall I said, "Reverend Stegall...I...Er-r-r..." I stumbled all over my words not knowing what to say, still embarrassed by the idea of receiving money for preaching.

Because I had turned to Rev. Stegall, Ernest handed him a five-dollar bill. Stegall nodded graciously, and put it into his pocket. A little later, Stegall gave me the five dollars and told me to apply it to my school bill. Then he explained that usually an honorarium is given at a wedding and sometimes at funerals. After that formality was finished, Stegall left for home, and Ernest, Edith and I went back into the assembly area for refreshments.

Pushing the Bride Out the Window

Within a few minutes Ernest came to me. "We want you to go back with us to the office again," Ernest told me in all seriousness. The wrinkled brow and nervous hesitation in his voice told me something was wrong. When we returned to the office, he coolly announced to me, "My friends are going to steal Edith, you gotta help us escape."

Three of Ernest's drinking buddies were in the Sunday School assembly area enjoying the refreshments. They had positioned themselves where they could keep an eye on my office. I had seen them in the Sunday School area, so I said to Ernest, "If you go back out into the hall, they'll see you."

"Help me get Edith out of the window," Ernest begged.

Now that was a formidable task. Edith must have weighed 250 pounds plus, and at this time she was still in high heels, stockings and her "Sunday go-to-meeting dress." Little skinny me and tall lanky Ernest were supposed to help Edith get out of a church window and onto the ground. I tried to lift up the stained-glass window, but the old wood and the many coats of paint had blocked the possibilities. On hot days I was able to lift the window about two feet; that was enough for me to climb through. I knew, however, that Edith could never fit through that two-foot opening.

I grabbed a letter opener and tried to scrape the worn-out paint from the cracks between the stained-glass window and the window frame. I stood on the long pew in my office and scratched feverishly from the bottom to the top, then across the top, hoping to free the window.

Ernest and I pushed with all our might, and were able to lift the window another 12 inches. Now we had made a 36-inch space in the window, just enough to push Edith through to the outside.

She stuck her head out the window first, and put her knees up on the window sill. I saw an immediate problem. "She'll fall on her head," I alarmedly announced to Ernest. "She can't go out head first; let's back her out."

"Ernest, help me!" Edith [the bride] screamed. Then she lapsed into the lewdest profanity my tender ears had ever heard. Obviously, she had not learned those words in Vacation Bible School or Sunday School.

So we turned her around, and stuck her rear end out the window, her knees on the window sill.

"Hang on to her arms," I quietly commanded Ernest. "We'll have to lower her to the ground."

"Don't drop her."

It must have been painful. Buttons were popping off the front of her dress, and white chalky paint was smeared down the front of her dress. Ernest and I were hanging on with all our might as we slowly lowered her to the ground.

Under his breath I could hear Ernest chuckle, "She's a heavy one."

"You ought to know," I whispered back. "You married her, you picked her out."

When Edith was almost down to the ground, two of Ernest's buddies burst out the church door, ran over and grabbed her around the waist and pulled her from our grasp.

Like a sack of grits falling off the back of a wagon, it was not a graceful drop to the ground. Her legs buckled and she went straight down to a sitting position, dragging the two buddies onto the ground with her.

"Ernest, help me!" Edith screamed. Then she lapsed into the lewdest profanity my tender ears had ever heard. Obviously, she had not learned those words in Vacation Bible School or Sunday School.

Kidnapping the Bride

A 1947 DeSoto four-door sedan wheeled around the corner; it was spinning sand and the horn was blowing loudly. The back door flew open. Those who remember the 1947 DeSoto know that the back door opened forward. The two men dragged Edith, still screaming profanities, to the car. The driver was out of the car by this time, pushing her in while the other two laughing buddies were pulling.

"Go get her," I yelled to Ernest to save his true love.

"I can't jump out that window," he drawled in slow Georgia redneck fashion. "I'll break my leg."

Ernest turned to the office door—I had only one door to my office. The door knob would not turn; someone on the outside was holding it so Ernest could not open it. My office door had no lock on it, but some of the teenage boys who knew what was going on were jokingly helping out. They held the office door shut so Ernest and I could not leave.

Again the car began spinning sand as the motor roared for the escape. The driver honked the horn, and the accomplices were leaning out the window laughing, waving and yelling as they drove down Alexander Street away from Westminster Presbyterian Church. When the teenage boys knew that the get-away car was out of reach, they released the office door. Ernest and I emerged to laughs and ridicules of the other wedding guests.

How does one describe laughter? Sometimes people laugh because of pity, or they laugh because it is unexpected or they laugh in ridicule. The room was filled with mixed laughter. It was a big joke to the teenage boys; obviously, the teenage girls were yelling in disapproval.

I was embarrassed. Although I had not been a part of the kidnapping, I was in the room when it took place. I was trying to help Edith and Ernest's escape, and I had seen the whole scenario unfold before my pure eyes. I like to control everything and wanted a dignified church with respectable people. Instead, I got a neighborhood full of common folks who enjoyed one another, and enough young men in the neighborhood who enjoyed kidnapping the bride.

I could do nothing, so I learned very early that when you can't do anything, don't try to do anything.

I do not know what happened for the next 10 or 15 minutes—my memory is blurred. By the time the festivities had ended, however, the greenery and potted plants had been removed from the auditorium and the Sunday School area had been cleaned.

Observations of an Absurd Evening

I went out the front door and there was Ernest sitting dejectedly on the church steps. His head was in his hands and he looked uncomfortable in a suit and white shirt, which he rarely wore. He was a pathetic sight sitting on the church steps—a church he rarely attended.

"I am sorry," I said in my ministerial condolence.

"That's all right," Ernest explained to me. "We always steal the bride; she'll be all right."

Ernest went on to explain that he had stolen the bride of one of the guys, and his buddy was just paying him back for his dastardly deed. What was fun for Ernest on a similar night months before was now fun for the former forlorn groom who was paying back Ernest for his earlier misdeeds.

"Whatcha gonna do?" I stood in the warm Savannah evening, waiting for a cool breeze.

"Well, I'll just sit here, they'll bring her back," Ernest told me.

Ernest went on to explain that Edith would be all right with his friends. Obviously, I was concerned about sexual impropriety—again my pure mind was reflecting those thoughts. I do not remember how I asked Ernest if she would be all right in the presence of his friends. He assured me they would just get her drunk and keep her out for two or three hours.

"She'll be back."

As I walked around the corner of the church, I looked back and saw Ernest sitting in the light of those streetlights that had recently been installed. I walked to the back of the church for my bicycle, and after I rolled up my pant leg and stuck my Bible in my belt, I rode off in the opposite direction. I did not want to see Ernest again because I did not know what to say. It was a sad sight to see a new groom—his wife kidnapped—sitting on the church steps. Because I did not like sadness, I did not want to see the sight again.

PRINCIPLES TO TAKE AWAY

1. *The listening principle.* Many things in life we do not know; no matter how brilliant or experienced we are, none of us knows everything. It is best to listen, for we can learn many things when other people talk. When we ask questions too soon, or show our ignorance too soon, we lose the respect of other people.

2. *The principle of serenity found in absurdity.* To me the whole evening was absurd; and yet to my parishioners, it was a way of life. Young men played their games and tried to steal the new bride all in jest because it had been done to them. As I look back, these people had a deep respect for the institution of marriage. None of the young people in the church would have run away to get married or had the wedding in their homes. They wanted to be married in the church and wanted God's blessing on their marriages.

3. *The principle of the strength of tutors.* When beginning a task that is too big for you, seek a tutor who can guide you through the impossibilities and help you solve the unknowable problems. As long as there are young ministers, there will be elderly pastors who will teach them what to do.

"Smiling at an impossible situation"

5

The Toilet Paper Incident

One of the most difficult tasks for a young pastor is to delegate. For one thing, he is too young and inexperienced. He has always been taught to do things for older people, let them go first and be self-reliant. For another thing, when beginning to pastor, the person thinks he should know everything, do everything, be everywhere and provide anything anybody wants. As a result, young pastors sometimes run ambulance services to the hospital for the poor, baby-sit with the senile, and some parishioners will let them deliver their groceries.

I would never have thought providing toilet paper for a little boy would be a theological issue, a crucial issue, a little boy-saving issue.

Let me explain why providing toilet paper for a little boy became traumatic. My Sunday mornings at Westminster Presbyterian Church were hectic at best. Even the couple of minutes I had between Sunday

School and the worship service to review my message were sometimes interrupted, which is what happened on this particular morning. As I was dashing to my office, a young mother asked me for toilet paper.

A Typical Sunday Morning Schedule

First, let's review one of my typical Sunday mornings. I usually arrived at the church around 8:00 A.M., prayed and studied my message while no one was at the church. Promptly at 9:00 A.M. I went to the front hall, opened the narrow door to the left, climbed even narrower steps to an obscure landing (not quite a second story), and began ringing the bell to call people to Sunday School.

Ding-a-ling, ding, ding-a-ling, ding, ding-a-ling.

Each Sunday morning I altered the cadence to a different rhythm and meter, for no other reason than just to be different.

In the summer, I made sure the windows were all open and the fans were turned on. We did not have air-conditioning, only an oscillating fan on the platform that faced the audience until I began to preach. Then the fan was turned on me—perhaps to cool down the sermon. In the winter, I had to make sure the floor furnace was lit and the church was warm. Because the church was old the Sunday School rooms were not heated, so the oscillating fan was placed in the hallway to blow down heat into those rooms.

People began arriving at church around 9:45 A.M. I was a Sunday School superintendent who conducted opening exercises. I began by rousingly and emphatically leading the singing for three hymns.

"Let's sing as loud as we can," I encouraged the group.

After the hymn, I led in prayer.

Then I made the announcements and called for all those who had birthdays to come forward and drop their pennies into the birthday cake, which was really a bank. The bank was just a plastic cake that had plastic candles placed on the top and a slot for inserting the money. Each person came to drop into the slot the amount of pennies equal to his or her birthday; then I led everyone in singing the happy birthday song.

Each class taught the "International Uniform Lesson," so the Scripture lesson printed on a one-sided sheet was distributed to all those who were present. I led in responsive reading; I read the first verse, the congregation repeated in unison until we completed the Scripture passage.

Then I usually dismissed in prayer, each person going to his or her classroom. After that I taught the junior boys in my classroom overlooking the front porch.

How It Happened

It happened as I was leaving my junior boys' class to make a mad dash down the hall to my office. I had just closed the class in prayer, and the confrontation took place in the hallway between the junior classroom and my study. It could not have taken place at any other location in the church because the men's rest room was located between my office and the junior classroom.

The rest room was old. The commode was old, the kind that had the water tank attached up on the wall; and to flush the toilet a lit-

---

A lady came out of the men's rest room——that's right, a lady came out of the men's rest room. The young mother held open the door. "There's no toilet paper in the men's room."

---

tle chain was pulled, which made the water rush through the pipe into the commode. Because the rest room was long and narrow, someone had purchased a long flat basin, and I always remember that it was too high for little boys to reach.

A lady came out of the men's rest room—that's right, a lady came out of the men's rest room. The young mother held open the door.

"It's all right," she assured me in her matronly voice, pointing inside to her little boy sitting on the throne. Then dramatically she dropped her voice and whispered, "There's no toilet paper in the men's room."

Panic hit me. Rather than facing the problem, gathering all the data, surveying the possible solutions and thinking of a workable answer, panic clogged all my arteries. I did not know what to think. I did not know what to do. I knew, though, that someone had to do something, and because I was the pastor I thought it had to be me.

My first reaction was to tell the woman to find a newspaper, wad it up to make it soft and use it. That was an admission of defeat, though, because it would make our church rest room look like the country outhouse back on the farm. I could not bring myself to tell her that.

Then the brilliant thought hit me—the women's rest room. Forcing a wide smile from here to eternity, I said, "Look in the ladies rest room, there will be some in there."

The young mother began shaking her head negatively before I got the words out of my mouth, and looked at me in a disgusting way as though I should understand what was happening. Her dismay suggested that I did not know what was going on, or did not care.

She announced, "I've already been there; that's why we're in the little boys' room."

She stood—waiting.

I stood—not knowing what to do.

The longer she waited, the more nervous I became.

My Inability to Find a Solution

I began to think about toilet paper, and realized the corner store was a block and a half away. I was young and fast, and if I broke into a dead run I could reach the store, buy the toilet paper and return just about the time I should walk onto the platform for the morning service. My feet told me, go, go, go.

For some reason, caution held me back. I resisted the impulse of breaking into a dead run. One of the reasons was my perceived image of importance in the community. What would everyone think of the pastor in a dark suit running down the street at breakneck speed to the local store? I could hear the discussion the following morning at Mrs. Smith's house.

I could hear her telling a neighbor, "You should have seen the pastor sprinting down the street in breakneck speed to the store to get toilet paper for a little boy."

They would laugh.

I was embarrassed just thinking about the possibility.

I wish this story had a happy ending, or a funny ending or any ending at all. The problem is now I am past 60 years old and I can't remember everything I did when I was 19.

At the time, my emotions exploded with an imperative to find some toilet paper for the woman; yet I have developed a clogged drain to my memory tubes. I don't remember what I did.

I could have said, "Some lady must have a Kleenex packet in her purse, let's check that out." But I did not think of that because I was emotionally embarrassed.

I could have said, "Let me get one of the ushers or elders to help you out. I have to prepare for the sermon." But I didn't. I didn't try to summon help.

I could have said, "Mrs. Yarborough lives right next door to the

I had an improper view of what the pastor was supposed to do—certainly an inadequate view. If I was psychologically immature— and I certainly was—the toilet paper issue became a crisis to help me grow up and let others help me in ministry.

church, I am sure she would loan us a roll of toilet paper." But I didn't think of getting help from Mrs. Yarborough.

My Inability to Delegate

Why was the toilet paper issue so crucial in my thinking? Why can't I remember its solution? In the first place, the emergency was a teaching moment for a young pastor. I had not learned how to delegate tasks to others; nor had I learned the role of sharing ministry with the men or women in the church.

I also had an improper view of what the pastor was supposed to do—certainly an inadequate view. If I was psychologically immature—and I certainly was—the toilet paper issue became a crisis to help me grow up and let others help me in ministry.

Pride Was Involved

Another factor was involved. Plain old pride and ego was crouching in the hallway to pounce on me that Sunday morning. I was too proud to search for help, so I did not want to ask someone for help. I was too proud to suggest she use just any old paper. I was too proud to ask her to borrow a Kleenex packet from someone else. Certainly, I was too proud to dash headlong through the neighborhood to the local store. The fact that I even thought of these possibilities, and their problems, tells how much pride was involved in the issue.

What ever happened right after the toilet paper incident? I do not remember. I seemed to get along all right. I did look over my notes and I went to the pulpit and preached that morning. Did God do a greater work that morning because He had humbled me? I doubt it. Did the lady's question about the toilet paper distract me so much that I preached a poor sermon? I doubt it.

The church service flowed smoothly, the people left that morning without any sign of distress and the lady continued to come back to the church. I suppose her son was cleaned up one way or another.

Learn to Say "I Can't Help You"

When I think about the toilet paper incident, I think about all the things in life pastors are asked to do. Pastors should do what they can, and what is in keeping with their tasks and the goals of the church. They should do what they can to help people, to relieve suffering and to fulfill the example of Jesus.

Pastors, however, need to learn these magical words: "I can't help you." They need to offer suggestions such as, "But I am sure someone else can help you," or "I'll try to get help for you." Pastors should remember they are human, very human, and they are vulnerable, very vulnerable to pride and a "Messianic complex" that makes them think they can do everything. Next time you are faced with an impossible question from an exasperated person, remember the toilet paper incident in the life of Elmer Towns, and smile. I do.

PRINCIPLES TO TAKE AWAY

1. *The principle of separating self from the office.* Too often pastors have their self-esteem and their self-perception all mixed up with the office God has given them. They need

to disassociate their personal feelings from their professional tasks and be able to say, "I can't help you." Then say, "Let me find someone to help you."

2. *The servanthood principle.* Pastors will be asked to perform many tasks they think are beneath them. Although I was frustrated by being asked about toilet paper, consider a second side to that humorous event. Of all the people in the church, the young mother came to me first, and me only. Whether I could have done something, or should have done something, it was commendable that she told me she needed toilet paper for her son. Her request might have revealed the attitude of the church toward me—they trusted me. That trust was the basis for some of my success at Westminster Presbyterian Church.

3. *The dignity principle.* Although we may at times detach ourselves from the office of pastor, we should do nothing to bring discredit to that office. The word "pastor" derives from *poimen*, which is shepherd, and a pastor is a shepherd of people. Christ is the shepherd of the Church and each human pastor serves under Jesus Christ; and in his human limitation should do nothing to bring disdain to the office. When I think of all the things I wanted to do that Sunday morning, and might have done, I am glad for each of those things I did not do. I did retain the dignity of the man of God, and thus could stand at an open coffin and preach the gospel, as well as stand in front of young couples to perform a wedding ceremony. The congregation could look up to the office and, in some ways, the man who filled the office.

"Learning about the power of prayer"

6

I Haven't Had
Healing 201 Yet!

It was Saturday night and I had just gone to sleep. My sermon
was prepared for the next day, the bulletin was done and as far as
I knew, everything was ready for God to touch the people in West
Savannah the next day. I had no anxiety in my sleep, but the
tension I would face in the next two hours would change my life
and teach me something about how God heals people in this
present age.

The phone rang.

Little did I know that the phone call would confront me with a
major theological issue I had no training to handle—healing. Before
the night ended, I would be asked to heal someone—something I
had never done. I would be asked to lay hands on the sick—something I had never seen done.

I haven't taken Healing 201, I later thought. I was just a junior in Bible college.

The demanding phone rang incessantly, awakening everyone in the darkened house. Immediately I was out of bed and stumbled toward the dining room. I experienced panic in my mind. No one phoned the Towns residence this late at night, except in an emergency.

Who died? I thought. *Maybe someone had an accident.*

My mind raced to the emergency room at the hospital. A lot of people in my parish became drunk on Saturday night, and inebriated people cause a lot of problems.

"What's wrong?" I heard my mother yell through the darkness as I picked up the phone.

"This is Mrs. Van Brackle," I heard the scratchy voice of an elderly woman whispering through the receiver. Without exchanging pleasantries, she told me a detailed story of what had happened that afternoon.

Devastated by a Faith Healer

A famous faith healer had set up his tent in Charleston, South Carolina, 120 miles away. Mrs. Van Brackle told me that if she could get to his tent, the faith healer would cure her cataracts. At age 82, she was almost blind. She persuaded her two grandsons to drive her to Charleston. The boys—older than I was at the time—were not church attenders. They did not drive their grandmother 120 miles because they thought she would be healed. They were skeptical of the whole thing, but they did it anyway. They just did it to please her.

Mrs. Van Brackle arrived at the tent two hours early, filled out the card and was interviewed by an associate evangelist. Then this elderly woman who could barely see was placed in the healing line. She stood patiently, waiting for the meeting to start, then waited through the sermon, then waited for her opportunity to go up on the platform. She finally reached the platform.

"Reach both hands to heaven," the faith healer exhorted.

She reached for heaven.

"Heal!" he loudly commanded, thumping her on the forehead.

"Can you see?" he inquired.

"No."

He repeated the process a second time and with imploring

expectancy, again asked, "Can you see?"

"No."

Then the faith healer began the process a third time.

"Reach higher."

Mrs. Van Brackle was reaching as high as she possibly could, praying with all her heart, so intently she was afraid her heart would stop beating.

"No," she sincerely told the faith healer, slowly shaking her head from side to side. "I can't see at all."

"It's your lack of faith," he barked. "Woman, it's your lack of faith."

When the faith healer told Mrs. Van Brackle her lack of faith was the problem, he devastated her. She crumpled under his touch, and the associate evangelist helped her to the platform's edge. The two grandsons took her to the car and did not stay for the rest of the tent revival meeting.

The Preacher Comes to the Rescue

All the way home Mrs. Van Brackle told her grandsons, "I'll call my preacher, he'll help me."

She arrived back in West Savannah after 10 o'clock at night. She did not consider how late it was. She told me the whole story on the phone, detail by detail, head blow by head blow.

"I gotta talk to you tonight," she pleaded.

As a young preacher, I thought I had to respond immediately every time my people called. Today, I might not go to see her. Back then, I reacted that night and I am glad I did because I grew in grace more than I helped her.

Racing to One of My People

As a 20-year-old pastor, I felt the need to impress people. This meant being appropriately dressed every time I did my pastoral duties. My age was a hindrance to rational thinking. So I turned on a night light and slipped on a white starched shirt and quickly tied a Windsor knot in my tie. I finished dressing and slipped out the back door to my racing bike.

I rode my English racing bike all around Savannah when I pastored Westminster Presbyterian Church. I locked it to the gas meter at Candler Hospital or just left it at the front door of my parishioners' houses.

I rolled up my pant leg to keep the cuff out of the greasy chain. I then stuck my Bible under my belt next to my stomach. It was seven miles across town to Mrs. Van Brackle's house, and pushing hard, I knew I could be there in 35 minutes.

All the way to Mrs. Van Brackle's house, I fretted about what she had said on the phone. The famous faith healer could not heal her, so how could I? Beyond that, however, I was not sure I believed in faith healers or faith healing. I knew God answered prayer and when a person prayed sincerely, God honored the request in His own time and in His own way.

Do I correct her doctrine, or do I show sympathy? I thought.

Mrs. Van Brackle lived in what was called a "shot gun" house by the people in Savannah. It earned the title "shot gun" because a hall ran from the front door straight to the back door and a shot gun could be fired through the house without hitting anything.

Greeting the Beer-Guzzling Grandsons

After I arrived, I entered the house and walked down the hall toward the kitchen on the left. The two grandsons were each holding an open bottle of beer and had been sitting around the kitchen table talking about me. They were half drunk on beer by this time.

One of the grandsons asked, "Think you can heal her?"

I smiled sheepishly. I was more intimidated than anything else. I did not try to witness to them, or tell them they should not drink. I did not know what to say. I just grinned and we exchanged a few pleasantries.

I feared false expectations. I did not know what they expected of me and I did not know what I could do, or not do. I just grinned, and they grinned, too.

A Surprising Request

I walked past the kitchen and headed to the last bedroom on the left. The small room looked like a shed rather than a bedroom because the rafters were exposed. The room had formerly been a back porch, but was now enclosed.

"Good evening, Mrs. Van Brackle," I greeted her as I entered the room.

I did not want an audience, but the two half-drunk grandsons followed me into the room. I had no idea what I would do, or what I would say, but I sure did not want any spectators if I messed up.

Mrs. Van Brackle lifted herself up on one arm. Her stringy gray hair was disheveled and her eyes were hollow. Whether it was the strain of the day, the late evening or she had pain in her eyes, she seemed tired.

The room smelled musty. It was not the smell of old people, or the smell of dirt, but the musty smell of wet wash in the basket waiting to be hung out to dry. It had rained that day and the room and the walls felt damp and musty.

I expected Mrs. Van Brackle to ask me to heal her, or at best to ask me to pray for her. She did not request either one.

A Question of Faith

In a whispering voice Mrs. Van Brackle said, "The man told me I didn't have any faith." She spoke as she lifted her body higher off the bed.

Then repeating herself, she emphasized each word, "The...man...said...I...didn't...have...faith." She paused.

Although I was young and not wise about many issues, I knew when to keep quiet. I looked at Mrs. Van Brackle intently and she

---

Mrs. Van Brackle asked, "How can I have faith?" I was preparing an answer about healing or the ethics of faith healers. Her question caught me by surprise and my computer shut down. The screen went blank.

---

looked back at me. I did not look at the two half-drunk grandsons because I did not know how to react to them. Although I would not look at them, I could feel their eyes penetrating the back of my head.

The room turned strangely silent. She stared and said nothing and I looked back and said nothing. I could hear hard nasal breathing from one of the grandsons. Rain dripped from the roof's edge into a puddle on the ground.

Then Mrs. Van Brackle's peppy voice broke the silence and she asked a question. She did not ask me to heal her, but asked, "How can I have faith?"

The simplicity of the question shocked me. My mind went blank. I was preparing an answer about healing or the ethics of faith healers. Her question caught me by surprise and my computer shut down. The screen went blank.

The nasal breathing behind me was heightened. I knew the grandsons wanted an answer. They had given up their Saturday to take their grandmother to be healed, and nothing had happened. They wanted an answer.

I was intimidated; I was frightened. So I did what most people do when they are scared—I prayed.

God, give me an answer.

It was a quickly breathed silent prayer. I did not want to let Mrs. Van Brackle down and I wanted God to speak to her grandsons.

Then as quickly as I prayed, God brought a memorized Scripture reference to my mind.

"Mrs. Van Brackle, if you want more faith," I explained carefully, "you need more Bible."

I then quoted Romans 10:17: "Faith cometh by hearing, and hearing by the word of God" *(KJV)*.

I told her what the verse meant: "When we get more Bible in our lives, we get more faith in our lives."

Illustrating How to "Get More Bible"

I explained to Mrs. Van Brackle an illustration I had heard in a class at Columbia Bible College. I held up five fingers of one hand and told her it took five fingers of one hand to hold a sword tightly (i.e., the sword being the Word of God). Then holding my Bible in front of her with five fingers, I told her it takes five fingers to hold the Bible properly.

Holding my Bible with my little pinkie finger, I showed her how the Bible would drop out of my hand. I explained that the little finger represented hearing the Bible.

Then holding my Bible with my ring finger, I explained that the ring finger represented reading the Bible. "Two fingers are better than one."

I explained that the tall finger represented studying the Bible, and the pointer finger represented memorizing the Bible. The thumb represented meditating on the Bible.

I held my Bible with all five fingers that late Saturday evening, explaining that she would grow in her faith by doing all five things: hearing, reading, studying, memorizing and meditating on God's Word.

"The more the Bible gets into you and controls you and becomes your passion, the more faith you will have," I told Mrs. Van Brackle.

We talked awhile. Then I turned to the two grandsons and

I quietly thought, What will the elders of the church say when they hear about this? I've never heard of a Presbyterian laying hands on people.

shared the plan of salvation with them, but did not press them to receive Christ that evening.

Then turning to Mrs. Van Brackle, I told her, "Before leaving, I want to pray for you."

Mine was a simple request any pastor makes of parishioners, but her response shocked me.

A Presbyterian Laying Hands On a Parishioner

"Will you lay hands on my eyes and ask God to heal me?" she asked.

Again I panicked. I thought I had walked through a minefield unhurt, but this request was something else. I had never seen a preacher lay hands on someone for healing. I was not sure it was supposed to be done. I knew Pentecostals did it, but I had never seen Presbyterians do it. My initial reaction was that I did not want to do it.

The thought flashed through my mind, *People will think you have turned into a fanatic, or worse, a faith healer.* I wanted people to think I was respectable.

Mrs. Van Brackle closed her eyes and waited. I hesitated.

I quietly thought, *What will the elders of the church say when they hear about this? I've never heard of a Presbyterian laying hands on people.*

I decided what to do in 10 seconds, but I was thinking a thousand miles an hour.

I rationalized, *Jesus did it, but I'm not Jesus.*

Then I realized I had no reason *not* to do it. A settled peace fell on me, as purposefully as lemon is dropped into tea. I had no reason *not* to do it, so I reached out awkwardly, hesitantly, and lay my hands on Mrs. Van Brackle's eyes.

"Lord, You are the Great Physician. You can heal. If it be Your will, heal her." I prayed a typical Presbyterian prayer for sick people. I did not shout, I did not command, nor did I beg. In my heart, I knew I was talking to God and asking Him to heal Mrs. Van Brackle.

The Power of Prayer

After I ministered to Mrs. Van Brackle, I rode my bike home and forgot about the healing incident. The following day in church I did not mention having prayed for Mrs. Van Brackle; nor did I mention it in my college classes the following week. I did not ask prayer for her, nor did I pray for her again.

The following Saturday afternoon a small barefooted boy came to the church and told me Mrs. Van Brackle wanted to see me. I walked the one block from the church to her shotgun house. I thought it was more dignified to walk in the church's neighborhood than to ride my bicycle. When I knocked on her door no one came, so I entered and yelled down the hall. Mrs. Van Brackle was in the back room. When I walked into her room, she motioned for me to sit down next to her bed.

"Hand me the Bible," she requested. After I gave her the Bible, she opened it to the psalms and began to read Psalm 103:1 *(KJV)*.

"Bless the Lord, O my soul: and all that is within me, bless his holy name."

"What do you think of that?" Mrs. Van Brackle asked.

"It's fine," I innocently responded.

I did not realize what she was doing, nor did I realize the enormity of the situation. I had forgotten about the previous Saturday evening when I prayed for her. Perhaps I was too immature and involved in too many activities to realize what was happening.

"I can see," she laughed out loud. "I can read the Bible." Her now seeing eyes twinkled. "Your prayers healed me."

I was embarrassed at the conversation and became uneasy. I did not like the thought of anyone having power to pray for healing. I knew God healed, but I honestly knew that nothing in my heart did it. My prayers were not exceptional, my faith was not exceptional and I was not exceptional.

"I'm uneasy with that kind of talk," I told Mrs. Van Brackle. I even told her it might have been the faith healer—maybe a delayed reaction. She would have none of that conclusion.

"My preacher healed me," she later told her grandsons.

I did not tell anyone about my prayer for 30 years. I was afraid people would think I was bragging, or that I might have power and someone would ask me to pray for his or her cataracts, and the next time nothing would happen. I did not tell anyone, because I knew my prayers did not heal her, and I knew I did not have what the Bible says about the prayer of faith saving the sick (see Jas. 5:15).

God, however, seemed to use my sincerity and faithfulness to heal Mrs. Van Brackle. Because of her faith in me to heal her through God, and by "getting more Bible," she was able to see again. I was simply following my heart and doing what God inspired me to pray and do for her.

PRINCIPLES TO TAKE AWAY

1. *The principle of having a ready answer.* When I first entered Bible college, I began memorizing Scripture for my personal growth and to answer my questions about my faith. I thought if I had answers for my questions from God's Word, I would have answers for others. The Bible exhorts us to be ready with "an answer to every man that asketh you a reason of the hope that is in you" (1 Pet. 3:15, *KJV*). I was able to answer Mrs. Van Brackle because I had memorized Scripture.

2. *The principle of an unexpected phone call.* We never know when we might receive a phone call that will threaten us or dramatically change our lives. The phone call late one Saturday evening interrupted my schedule, but proved to be an experience whereby God exploded my faith and began to teach me about healing.

3. *The principle of following one's heart.* What should you do when you honestly do not know what to do? Not all people can follow their hearts, because some are committed to evil, have hardened their hearts or, at best, have no biblical witness in their hearts to tell them what God would have them do. If you have memorized the Scriptures, have yielded yourself to God and have prayed daily for God's guidance, however, then when you face difficulties you do not know how to handle, follow your heart.

7

A Deathbed Conversion

Death is one of the scariest experiences for a young preacher. I had officiated at a funeral, but I had no idea what to do in a hospital room of someone on the verge of death, especially an unsaved person, even an atheist. I was sent to St. Joseph's Hospital to witness to the only atheist in our neighborhood. Silla Hair expected me to convert him. I blundered into a situation and God helped me.

Mrs. Smith was one of the three ladies in the church whose last name was "Smith." She was, however, the only Mrs. Smith among the five ladies who had originally asked me to be their preacher at the mission Sunday School. She was also the quietest and most retiring of the ladies in the church.

Mrs. Smith had salt-and-pepper gray hair, wore an ever-present white apron around her pudgy middle and had one of the cleanest houses in the neighborhood. It would have been a warm comfy house, except for the dozens of potted plants on her front porch, and many dozens of potted plants placed everywhere in her living room. The house smelled like a florist shop and felt like a nursery. Mrs. Smith never invited me to her house for a meal; I just made pastoral visits in the living room.

Mr. Smith was never home when I visited.

Because Mrs. Smith was the quietest of all the ladies, she once meekly requested, "Please pray for my husband, he doesn't believe in God."

Hm-m-m-, I thought to myself, *how do I present the gospel to an atheist?*

Mr. Smith worked nights and slept days. I seldom saw him, but knew that he always wore a white shirt with sleeves rolled up past the elbows, and a straw hat. He was neither fat nor skinny, and had a Winston Churchill protruding middle.

Because Mr. Smith's job kept him unavailable to me, and I did not know how to share the gospel with an atheist, I never had an opportunity to witness to him.

A Gripping Call to the Hospital

Usually I took the young people of Westminster Presbyterian Church to Youth for Christ meetings on Saturday night; it was a good means of encouraging them spiritually. Because I was a single 19-year-old male, a lot of high school girls attended our church's youth meeting—a lot more girls attended than did boys. The mothers of the girls constantly invited me to their houses for meals and were always volunteering to chaperone the young people to their outings. So I never had any difficulty arranging for someone to drive the young people to the Youth for Christ meetings.

On this particular night, I had led the singing at the Youth for Christ meeting, and by my own egotistical estimation, I had done a pretty good job. After the meeting, we were all standing around fellowshiping, when suddenly Mrs. Silla Hair walked into the room by way of the back door.

Immediately, I knew something was wrong. Mrs. Hair was not the chaperone of the evening, but she brought a special message for me.

"Mr. Smith is in the emergency room at the hospital," Silla Hair said. "He had a heart attack...he's not expected to live...Mrs. Smith and the family are there now."

I told Mrs. Hair I would come to the hospital as soon as I possibly could.

"You can lead him to Christ." Mrs. Hair expressed great faith, much greater than mine.

When my pastoral compassion was centered on 45 to 50 homes, I could be specific in my deep feelings of anguish. Later, when I worked in a church of thousands and someone from the church had a physical emergency, it did not have the captivating "grip" on me when the same thing happened. I have not been "gripped" since the news about Mr. Smith captivated me that night.

I felt compelled to go to the hospital. Whether my feeling was guilt about not witnessing to Mr. Smith, or compassion because he lived in the neighborhood, or obligation because of my pastoral position—I do not know the reason. I knew I had to do something, though, but I did not know what I needed to do.

After the young people attending the Youth for Christ meeting were dropped off in West Savannah, I rode my English racing bike to the hospital. According to my usual practice, I hid it around the back and locked it to a gas meter. Then strolling around to the front of the hospital, holding my Bible, I tried to look as dignified as did all the other visiting clergy to St. Joseph's Hospital.

The hospital was a large, dark brick multistoried building located in downtown Savannah; it was old and foreboding and very Catholic. Right in the foyer stood a large pasty-pink statue of the Virgin Mary to remind us of the Roman Catholic oversight of the hospital. The dark green linoleum on the floors covered old wood, and as I walked through the hall the noise from my leather shoes ricocheted off the walls.

Tap...tap...tap...

A Young Preacher's Intimidation

The Smith family could hear me coming down the corridor, for I was the only activity in St. Joseph's cardiac-arrest center that evening. When I reached the family waiting room, I saw Mrs. Smith and approximately 12 people I did not know. These were her grown children and in-laws.

At age 19, I was the youngest looking in the room and probably the most immature. I was also the only one who looked uncomfortably out of place. I was wearing a white shirt and tie and my dark suit, and carried a very big Bible. Today, you would say I looked like a Mormon missionary because of my racing bicycle, white shirt and tie, and my Bible.

I boldly entered the dimly lit waiting room, walked around and shook hands with each man, introducing myself as Mrs. Smith's pastor. It was approaching midnight and they had been there since suppertime. They were tired and irritable, and many of them did not want to "coddle" the young preacher they thought had little to offer them.

"What can he say?" I heard one of them whisper to Mrs. Smith as I went over to talk with her, not knowing what to say.

By emotionally identifying with people, the pastor tends to become neurotic, and in his "codependency" relationship he abdicates from any help he may be able to give.

"He's not going to make it through the night," Mrs. Smith said seriously. "The doctor doesn't give him much chance of making it."

The news of Mr. Smith's imminent death compounded my problem. I did not have the slightest idea how to prepare a person to die, nor did I have a clue how to prepare a wife and children for the death of a husband and father. Neither did I know how to prepare myself.

My feelings for the people in West Savannah were personal; so much so that I felt deeply about every problem, death and failure. Every time one of the teens was arrested, or was in trouble at school, I took it personally. Because I was the pastor, I felt failure when anyone in the church failed. I thought I had let down the whole church when I could not lead someone to Jesus Christ. I thought they blamed me for my lack of spirituality.

For some reason I thought it would be my fault if Mr. Smith died. Today, I realize that a pastor must detach himself from the problems of his people so he can minister grace and help to the very people who need help. By emotionally identifying with people, the pastor tends to become neurotic, and in his "codependency" relationship he abdicates from any help he may be able to give. I did not understand that as a young pastor, however. I just threw my heart into the family waiting room, walked in as one of them and tried to help.

But who was going to help me?

I saw a deeper problem, though. I glanced around the waiting room from one unshaven face glazed with anxiety into the eyes of the next. I wondered how many of them were atheists. Mrs. Smith was a delightful lady, but not the dominant force in her home. I did not know about the strength of her husband's atheism, or how deeply each in the room was infected.

Preaching and Praying in the Waiting Room

"Would you like me to lead you in prayer?" my nervous voice squeaked to the people in the waiting room. I sensed a few seconds of tension as one middle-aged sibling exchanged glances with another.

Finally, one son said, "Mother would like that."

"Before I pray, I would like to read Scripture to all of you," I announced.

I quickly breathed a prayer that no nurse would interrupt me and that everyone would understand what I was reading. Then turning to John 3:7, I slowly read the passage of Jesus telling Nicodemus, "You must be born again," as I had explained the plan of salvation in home after home.

I explained very carefully what it means to be born again. This family all lived in the "Christianized" culture of the South, and knew hymns and religious terminology. They understood the Christmas message that Jesus was born of a virgin, and the Easter message that He had died for the sins of the world.

I had a deeper question for each of them, however: "Are you born again?"

Although I was young and intimidated by their perceived atheism, that evening in the hospital waiting room I boldly proclaimed the necessity for everyone's new birth. I explained that church membership was not enough, that belief in God was not enough and that faithful church attendance was not enough.

I pressed home the claim: "You must be born again."

Then I prayed. When you don't perceive yourself as a spiritual intercessor who can rattle the windows of heaven, how do you pray? I only knew one way to pray, and that was simply to open my heart to God. My prayer was unsophisticated, undignified and the words were ill framed. Nevertheless, I prayed from the bottom of my heart because I felt responsible for Mr. Smith's healing, and should he die, I thought I would be responsible for his death.

"God, heal Mr. Smith and raise him back up," I prayed boldly in front of everyone. It was not a prayer to show off my theology, but an honest desire for Mr. Smith to live. The rest of my prayer was couched in typical ministerial language: "If it be Thy will...Thou art the Great Physician...we commit him into Thy hands."

My Ministerial Persona Did Not Work

I left the family waiting room and walked to the nurse's station. I introduced myself to the head nurse and told her I wanted to see Mr. Smith.

"I'm his pastor," I said in a ministerial authoritative way.

The nurse wearing her starched white cap dipped her head and looked over the top of her glasses with a squinted eye and simply said, "Hum-m-m-m-m-m." Her tone of "Hum-m-m-m-m-m-" told me she did not think much of my ministerial persona.

"He's not expected to live, and he's unconscious," she spit the words out in crisp fashion. "He wouldn't know you even if we let you in," she explained. "We're not even letting his wife in to see him."

For the next three hours I waited in the waiting room with the family. No one talked much and most of the men smoked. I was uncomfortable, not knowing what to say. I was not good at small talk with men who had nothing in common with me. So I just sat there, wondering why I was there.

I ought to go home and get some sleep so I will be fresh for my sermon tomorrow, I thought.

I was compelled to stay, though, and I felt as though I were in school and the teacher said, "It's not time for recess." So I just sat there and reviewed my sermon in my head. I knew the Smith family wondered why I did not go home, and I wondered the same thing.

A Smiling Nurse Came to the Rescue

At approximately 3:00 A.M., the head nurse who had looked over her glasses saying "Hum-m-m-m-m-m" to me announced that she was going home. She introduced her replacement, a much younger nurse who knew how to smile.

I stepped out of the waiting room to the nurse's station to explain to the much younger smiling nurse that I was the pastor, and that I wanted to see Mr. Smith. I explained that he was not saved, and I did not want him to slip into eternity without knowing God.

"I go to a Baptist church," the young smiling nurse said to me. She indicated an understanding of my spiritual problem. "I'll see what I can do."

I slipped back into the waiting room and was tremendously hopeful. Whereas the previous three hours had been filled with anxiety and frustration, now for the first time that evening I was hopeful. This young Baptist nurse understood why I was there, and would shortly let me in to see Mr. Smith, even though his wife was not permitted inside the room.

My faith was rewarded because shortly the smiling nurse stuck her head into the waiting room and said to me, "You can see Mr. Smith now."

Then to some surprised in-laws, and a few nonapproving in-laws, the nurse announced, "Even though he's not conscious, you can pray over him."

I thought, *That's a strange expression, "to pray over someone."* I entered the emergency room where Mr. Smith was lying in bed.

In the '50s, a heart-attack victim was kept in an oxygen tent, and air was pumped into a clear plastic tent covering the whole bed, not directly into the nostrils, as is done in later-day technology. The dimly lit table lamp was the only light in the room, and the dark shadows in the corners added a mystical effect to the setting. The slow hiss of oxygen into the tent compounded the threatening tone. The large red NO SMOKING sign seemed unnecessary.

Explaining Salvation to a Dying Man

The smiling Baptist nurse had seen Catholic priests administer last rites on many occasions, so I guess she wanted me to give the equivalent of Protestant last rites. She went to stand at the foot of the bed and bowed her head slightly, waiting for me to do my ministerial thing. I did not have a clue, however, what Protestant last rites were, and I had never heard of Roman Catholic last rites.

Not knowing what to do, I did what I had always done in a hospital room. I said, "Mr. Smith, can you hear me?"

His eyes were closed and he was deathly still. Then he slightly moved an arm, and to the shock of the nurse, nodded his head yes. I explained to him that while waiting in the waiting room I had prayed for him, his wife and his children.

"Do you understand what I have done?"

He nodded his head yes.

Then opening my Bible again to John 3:7, I told him what Jesus said to Nicodemus: "You must be born again." Just as I had done hundreds of times in hospitals and homes in West Savannah, I explained what it meant for a person to be born again.

At the end of each explanation I asked, "Do you understand me?"

Each time he nodded his head yes.

"Do you want to be born again, Mr. Smith?"

He nodded his head yes.

"Will you pray these words in your heart?"

He nodded his head yes.

"Dear God, I believe in You, I believe that Jesus was the Son of God, and I believe He died on the cross to save me from my sin."

After I had repeated that prayer, I asked Mr. Smith if he had prayed those words in his heart.

He nodded his head yes.

"Dear Lord, forgive me for my sin, forgive me for my smoking and drinking, forgive me for my cursing, forgive me for not going to church," I prayed. Then again to make sure, I asked if he had prayed those words in his heart.

He nodded his head yes.

"I pray this in the name of the Lord, Jesus Christ."

Again, he nodded his head yes.

I briefly explained to him how the dying thief on the cross went to heaven even though he believed just before death. Faith was all that was necessary to be saved.

Jesus said to the thief, "To day shalt thou be with me in paradise" (Luke 23:43, *KJV*). I explained to Mr. Smith that he was dying, and he had not been given any chance to make it through the night. I told him that if he had honestly asked Christ to come into his heart, that instantly upon death, he would go to heaven.

"To be absent from the body and to be present with the Lord" (2 Cor. 5:8).

Praying for Physical Healing

Then I thought, *I should pray for his physical healing.*

So I asked, "Do you want me to pray for God to heal you?"

He nodded his head yes.

I do not remember the content of this prayer. I do remember stretching out my hand and laying it on the plastic oxygen tent. I asked God to heal him of the heart attack, raise him up out of that bed, bring him home and put him into the church.

Keeping the Conversion Low Key

When I went back into the family waiting room, I told the family I had prayed for their father and husband, and that he had heard me. I told them he had nodded his head yes, that he could hear what I prayed. Because of the animosity I felt from the children, I did not tell them Mr. Smith had prayed to receive Jesus Christ. Neither did I tell Mrs. Smith. I decided I could tell her privately at another time.

As I left the hospital that night and rode my bicycle home, I was mentally preparing for Mr. Smith's funeral. I was trying to decide if I would tell the people beside an open grave that Mr. Smith had prayed to receive Jesus Christ right before his death. I was not sure I should make that announcement publicly, however; the people might think I was just "grandstanding." I did not have any way to verify what Mr. Smith had done. I was not sure the neighbors would believe my claim without proof.

The next morning as I was preparing for my sermon, word was brought to me that Mr. Smith had not died during the night. I was requested to pray a special prayer for him in the morning worship service. That morning we prayed for Mr. Smith, but I did not mention to anyone that he had prayed to receive Christ as Savior.

Verifying the Conversion Experience

I went back to Columbia Bible College on Sunday, as usual, and the following week when I returned to West Savannah for my weekend ministry I asked about Mr. Smith. I wanted to know about the funeral or if I had arrived in time to officiate.

My ego really played tricks on me. I wanted to announce to the church that I had prayed for Mr. Smith's healing, and as a result God had healed him.

"He's much better," someone mentioned to me. "He'll be coming home sometime this week."

My ego really played tricks on me. I wanted to announce to the church that I had prayed for Mr. Smith's healing, and as a result God had healed him. I could not bring myself to say that because I would be taking the glory that belongs to God. On the flip side, however, if people understood what had happened that night, they might come to the church to be saved. I struggled about my feelings for a week, undecided what I should tell the congregation.

I visited Mr. Smith in his home three weeks after the heart attack. A bottle of oxygen was sitting beside him and a plastic cup had been placed over his nose and mouth. He was wearing flannel pajamas and sitting in the living room reading a magazine when I came in. Mrs. Smith came out of the kitchen to sit with us. She was wiping her hands on the ever-present white starched apron as she sat next to him.

I opened my Bible, and again read to the Smiths John 3:7 where Jesus told Nicodemus: "You must be born again."

I described to both the Smiths where and how Mr. Smith had prayed to receive Christ.

"Did you really mean it that night?" I asked him in front of his wife.

He nodded his head yes.

Mrs. Smith was not demonstrative. She did not smile, cry or respond; she just nodded her head in agreement.

Within a couple of months Mr. Smith started attending church and always sat with his wife. After the night in the hospital and his conversion, I don't remember him ever missing a church service. He never went back to smoking and drinking, and the next time we had a baptism service, he was sprinkled by Rev. Carroll Stegall.

Mr. Smith never went back to work, because of his physical condition, but he was constantly around the church helping with small tasks. He became one of our most dependable ushers, and I could spot him walking to church two blocks away. I knew it was him because of the straw hat he wore and the sleeves on his white shirt rolled up past his elbows.

PRINCIPLES TO TAKE AWAY

1. *The principle that a sincere decision gives power.* Because of my experience with Mr. Smith, I have always thought anyone can make an instantaneous decision at a crisis point in his or her experience, and that the person's life would be irrevocably changed. Whenever I have heard people say Christianity is just a philosophy or a psychological reinforcement, I think back to Mr. Smith in the oxygen tent nodding that he had just prayed to receive Jesus Christ. He turned away from the sins of which he repented in the oxygen tent. He demonstrated to me the efficacy of his conversion experience. I wonder if today I would ask a person in that condition to repent of outward sins (smoking or drinking) he might never have the opportunity to commit again. Although I do not know what I would do in the future, I know God responded positively to the outlandish request I made of Mr. Smith when I thought he was dying.

2. *The "John Calvin" principle.* John Calvin was the founder of Calvinism, which I interpret as God in His sovereignty working out all details, even to minor details, by His power and controlling design. Through the years I have said that when little things have worked together for the obvious glory of God, "John Calvin struck again." For in the salvation of Mr. Smith, a Baptist nurse allowed me to enter a room to pray over a body she thought was unre-

sponsive, and yet in the sovereign purpose of God, Mr. Smith awakened enough to hear me pray. Mr. Smith responded to Jesus Christ in a deathbed conversion and from that strength he revived physically, and lived for Christ spiritually.

3. *The principle of professionalism as a response.* Many times I did not respond as a pastor, but as a friend who had deep feelings for people. Although my friendly response was not always professional, perhaps the depth of my feelings triggered a "faith response" that touched God to intervene in the crisis of those to whom I ministered.

"Me—third from left—with gospel team"

8

Sensationalizing Mr. Sweeney's Son

Because I was such a young Presbyterian pastor, I did not know anything about the "unpardonable sin," who might commit it or how to handle its implications. When I was a college sophomore begging God to give me a church where I could preach on weekends, all I wanted was a platform for my sermons. Little did I know that people are attached to sermons, and a congregation would teach me more theology, Bible interpretation and solutions to biblical problems than I could ever learn in any classroom. I was about to learn about the unpardonable sin.

Remember, I pastored a church because I love to preach, and I was bold in the pulpit. In pastoral visiting and handling personal problems, however, I was reluctant because I was young and inexperienced.

Hearsay About the Unpardonable Sin

I was visiting in someone's home, sitting in the living room talking to the people about heaven and hell, when someone mentioned, "It is too bad about Mr. Sweeney's son going to hell."

Pow. The blunt statement that Mr. Sweeney's son had gone to hell hit me right between the eyes. I did not know how to cope with such a statement. I had no idea what he had done, and I was unsure what to say.

I thought, *How can anyone be sure another person has gone to hell?*

"It's too bad about Mr. Sweeney's son going to hell," one of the ladies said to me. She added, "He committed the unpardonable sin!"

My question was good enough for me, so I did not ask why Mr. Sweeney's son had gone to hell. Was he an alcoholic? Was he a fornicator? Was he a pervert? Had he stood up in a congregation to blaspheme God?

The issue of Mr. Sweeney's son dropped from my mind. I had a lot of other things to concern me. About a week later I was sitting in another parish member's home when I again heard the same conversation.

"It's too bad about Mr. Sweeney's son going to hell," one of the ladies said to me. Then she became a little more talkative. She added, "He committed the unpardonable sin!"

Pow. It hit me again. Not only had he gone to hell, but he had also committed the unpardonable sin. I had heard the phrase "unpardonable sin," but did not have a clue what it was.

"I see," I nodded my head, not knowing what else to do.

I vaguely remembered somewhere at Bible college we had discussed it, but I could not discuss it with the lady because I did not know what questions to ask. I was afraid if I said anything it would show my ignorance, and the last thing in life I wanted was for the people to know how ignorant their young pastor was. So I continued smiling, nodding my head knowingly, all the while not having a clue what we were talking about.

It happened another time. I was in one of the local stores drinking a Grapette—a small grape drink we could purchase for a dime. I laid my Bible on the soft-drink box and asked the store owner to visit Westminster Presbyterian Church. I told the owner we offered good singing and I thought pretty good preaching.

We chatted about two or three things, then I asked the store owner, "Have you been born again?"

Just as many people do when asked about their souls, he changed the subject. The owner seemingly did not want to face spiritual accountability, so he focused on Mr. Sweeney's son.

"Do you really think Sweeney's son lost his salvation and went to hell?" the owner asked.

"What do you mean?" I asked.

The owner was a safe person of whom to ask this question. It could not hurt me too much if I revealed any ignorance.

So I asked again, "What do you mean lost his salvation?"

"The Sweeney boy was a good boy..."

The pot-bellied owner wrapped his hairy arms around his protruding dirty white apron and continued, "The boy was christened, had a good godparent and went to Sunday School all the time..."

Then he described Sweeney's son: he had attended Sunday School and was respectful to his parents.

"I never remember him ever trying to steal one thing in the store," the proprietor explained.

I should have listened more carefully and asked deeper questions. Instead, I kicked the sand on my shoe against the wooden floor.

"Here, let me get that." The store proprietor came from the back of the counter carrying the broom to sweep my shoes clean. I realize now that I was not sensitive to him, because I began to give him reasons a saved person could not lose his salvation.

I said something like, "Once saved, always saved..." then quoted two or three Bible verses to support my view of eternal security.

"That may be so," the owner surmised with a grin, by this time picking his teeth with a toothpick. "But I have seen some good men do evil things, and God ought to stick 'em in hell."

Researching the Unpardonable Sin Theory

The following week back at Columbia Bible College, I decided I had heard enough. Finding a Bible dictionary, I looked up the topic, "Unpardonable Sin." The only verse I found directly related to the topic were the words of Jesus, "Wherefore I say unto you, All manner of sin and blasphemy shall be forgiven unto men: but the blasphemy against the Holy Ghost shall not be forgiven unto men. And whosoever speaketh a word against the Son of man, it shall be forgiven him: but whosoever speaketh against the Holy Ghost, it shall not be forgiven him, neither in this world, neither in the world to come" (Matt. 12:31,32, *KJV*).

Finding Various Views About the Unpardonable Sin

That week I found out that Christians are not uniform in how they interpret the unpardonable sin. Some believe the unpardonable sin is a heinous act whereby a person lifts his or her fists toward God in rebellion to curse God, and thus loses his or her salvation.

The dispensationalists believe that the unpardonable sin could be committed only during the physical life of Jesus Christ by those who attributed the miracles of Jesus to the devil.

Still another evangelist taught that continued rejection of Jesus Christ by unsaved people hardened the heart until it became unable to respond.

The view I liked best was that any person who died without receiving Jesus Christ as Savior committed a sin that was not pardonable, because God cannot pardon the sin of unbelief—it is the final rejection of Jesus Christ. Anyone who died without receiving Jesus Christ had committed a sin that could not be pardoned. Why? Because being dead, the person was beyond the time of choice.

I wrote down these views in the front of my Bible, along with some supporting Scripture references.

A couple of days later I was talking with one of the upperclassmen who lived down the hall from me at Columbia Bible College. I told him the story about the unpardonable sin. I believe this conversation was ordained of God because what the upperclassman told me actually was the root of my problem with Mr. Sweeney's son.

This student told me the Roman Catholic view. Roman Catholics teach that someone who commits a mortal sin leading to death, such as suicide, commits a sin so heinous to God that the person cannot be pardoned. At the time I did not give much credibility to this position because I did not believe in the Roman Catholic view. I was armed with some facts, however, so I had, as they say, my gun loaded and ready.

An Unexpected Opportunity to Hear the Real Story

I did not walk around looking for an opportunity to discuss the unpardonable sin. As a matter of fact, I put it out of my mind and forgot about my research.

In the providence of God, however, a couple of weeks later I was visiting in the home of an elderly lady, who said, "It was a shame about the Sweeney's boy committing the unpardonable sin."

Quicker than an unexpected flat tire, the question popped out of my mouth.

"How did he die?"

The lady began a detailed explanation. The boy had put his father's shotgun into his mouth and with one of the toes on his right foot had pressed the trigger, blowing the top of his head against the wall.

I am not sure whether Westminster Church believed Mr. Sweeney's boy committed the unpardonable sin because of the influence of Roman Catholicism in Savannah, Georgia. Maybe it was the strong five-point Calvinism belief by some in the church, which teaches that anyone who kills himself is not saved in the first place. The people in my community ignorantly believed that if a person takes his or her life, that person is not converted (i.e., that person goes to hell).

I listened politely as the lady told me all the grisly details of the Sweeney boy's afternoon suicide. She told how people had heard the gun blast, and they came standing around the house waiting for the ambulance attendants to bring out the body. She went on to describe the morbid funeral. She told me how a depressed young man who had mental problems and many failures took his own life. I did not recognize the name of the minister who preached the sermon, but she said everyone in the community listened carefully.

Then she explained, "The minister didn't say that Sweeney's son went to heaven." Then she repeated, "We listened very carefully to see what he would say, and he didn't say that Sweeney's son went to heaven."

My Sermon Topic:
Why Mr. Sweeney's Son Went to Heaven

Young preachers not yet 20 years old are sometimes more bold than wise, more enthusiastic than mature, more motivated by foolhardy ego than by faith grounded in love for people.

My sermon topic the next Sunday would be: Why Mr. Sweeney's Son Went to Heaven. Metaphorically, I was out on a limb with a saw. That saw would either kill me or cause me to soar to new heights.

I went around the community telling people what my sermon topic the next Sunday would be: Why Mr. Sweeney's Son Went to Heaven.

Now that I look back on my public announcement, I was not sensitive to the Sweeneys or the grief they had suffered. I had not even told them I was planning to use them for a spectacular message.

"Whatcha going to preach on?" a man drove by me, slowed his car and yelled out the window to me.

"You'd better come and hear," I shot back using the same challenging tone he had given the question.

Obviously, the Sweeneys did not come to church the Sunday I based my sermon on the topic: Why Mr. Sweeney's Son Went to Heaven. The grief was probably too much for them, and they wisely stayed away. I should have known I was treading on thin ice. The elders who came to pray with me every Sunday before the sermon did not come that Sunday. I had to pray by myself.

Metaphorically, I was out on a limb with a saw. That saw would either kill me or cause me to soar to new heights.

Anyone who has heard me preach knows that today I tend to be more academic than emotional. Although my emotional topic and the emotional experience was about Sweeney's son, I still approached my sermon that day from an academic orientation.

A Passionate Presentation

In my sermon, I announced the five views I had learned about the unpardonable sin. I asked the people to listen carefully to all five views, and at the end of the sermon I would ask them to decide which view is right.

Not being very original, I presented the views exactly as I had discovered them in the dictionaries and commentaries. The last view I presented was the Roman Catholic view.

"Only Catholics believe Sweeney's son went to hell!"

I was young, I paused for effect, not knowing how thin the ice really was or what terrible repercussions I had produced in my congregation.

"If you think Sweeney's boy went to hell because he committed suicide..." I emphatically said.

Then I repeated the phrase again, and answered my own question, "You're wrong!"

Then I asked, "If I could show you one person in the Bible who committed suicide and went to heaven, who we know went into the presence of God, would you change your mind about Mr. Sweeney's son?"

I told them of Samson, the adulterer who was addicted to sexual sins, who died in a backslidden state by crushing the Philistine temple down upon his head.

"Surely this is an act of suicide," I announced authoritatively.

Then I turned to God's hall of fame—Hebrews 11. There right in the middle of the hall of fame is Samson's name.

Waxing bold again, I pronounced, "If Samson who committed sexual sins, if Samson who broke his Nazirite vow, if Samson who killed himself went to heaven, surely Sweeney's boy went to heaven."

At this point in the sermon, I turned from a correcting prophet to a compassionate minister preaching a eulogy at a funeral. I began to talk about all the good things the Sweeney boy had done. He had won Sunday School pins for faithful attendance, had memorized Scripture, had not stolen one thing from the community store and had made a decision for Jesus Christ at the Presbyterian Laurel Walker Camp in Waycross, Georgia.

"If a person sincerely has accepted Jesus Christ as his Savior, that person will go to live with Jesus upon death," I said with finality. "The Bible guarantees it."

Then exuding wisdom beyond my years, I explained that mental disease was not something for which the boy was accountable, and that God would not punish a person because he had a disease for which he was not accountable. This boy had been so severely depressed that it haunted him, driving him to take his own life.

A Personal Pulpitry Triumph

The sermon was a personal triumph in pulpitry. People talked about the sermon about as long as I pastored in the community. They admired it, and appreciated my setting the record straight. As far as I know, no one ever said again that Sweeney's boy went to hell because he committed the unpardonable sin. Notice, I said it was a personal triumph, but no one came forward in the church to be saved that day. I don't know, however, if it was a triumph for God.

I don't remember how I gave the invitation that Sunday, whether I was bold or reticent. I don't remember whether I was a flaming evangelist asking people to come forward, or a sympathetic minister at a funeral. All I remember is that I saw no visible results that day, nor do I remember anyone later coming to Christ because of that sermon.

The Sweeneys and I never talked about my sermon based on their son's death. No way was I going to ask them, "What did you think about my sermon?" Although they did not attend church that day, I am sure they heard about it from those who did. I had enough common sense to leave well enough alone.

Although I sensationalized the Sweeneys' son and they probably did not appreciate the way I focused on him for a sermon, in my heart I believe they must appreciate that I set the community straight about the unpardonable sin and the fact that people thought their son had gone to hell.

PRINCIPLES TO TAKE AWAY

1. *The principle of wise silence.* Sometimes when you don't know what people are talking about, and you don't have a

basis for asking a question, it is better to keep quiet. Then go study the matter and find out what they are talking about; the next time the issue surfaces, ask your questions.

2. *The principle of reflective repentance.* Today I would not preach a sensational sermon about a person's private problems. I would not sensationalize the people of my congregation. What I did in naiveté was motivated by impulsive youthfulness. God may have used the sermon, but today I would inform the community differently.

3. *The principle of researched opinion.* When you are not sure how to answer a question or problem, study the Scriptures and find out what godly people have said about the problem. When you have gathered enough relevant information, you are then prepared to handle the problem.

"The Bible-toting 'Preacher'"

9

Losing the War of the Streetlights

Nothing in life is absolutely black or white; most of it is gray. We live between perfect dreams and perfect fears. As a young pastor I would be confronted with an alternative, and I determined to fight it to death. "Compromise" was not a user-friendly term in my vocabulary.

"I'll not use my church pulpit for the projects of liberals, or do-gooders; there is no place in Westminster Presbyterian Church for the social gospel."

This was the essence of a sermon I preached, and within a few weeks, my convictions would be tested. Would I stick by my words, or eat my words?

A City Official's Challenge

I was eating supper at my mother's house around 4:30 P.M., when the phone call came.

The voice at the other end was a city official, who said, "Reverend Towns, I would like to ask..."

Before he could continue, I cut him off abruptly. I was not yet ordained so I would not let anyone call me "Reverend." I thought it was hypocritical.

"Just call me 'Preacher,'" I told the city official. "Everybody at the church calls me 'Preacher.'"

I could tell he was uncomfortable using the title "Preacher." It was not a term in his ecclesiastical vocabulary. Nevertheless, we continued to talk.

"I've had a hard time finding you," he explained, "but Mr. Seckinger told me where I could reach you."

Mr. Seckinger was the chairman of the board of elders at Westminster Presbyterian Church, and he and I did not always see "eye-to-eye" about many issues. Mr. Seckinger did not like my revivalistic preaching. He had a reputation of taking a few drinks, as well as slipping in a cussword once in a while. He and I had also experienced a few unpleasant confrontations. I did not warm up when the city official used the magical name, "Mr. Seckinger."

"If we get enough signatures on a petition, your neighborhood could get streetlights around the church," the city official stated.

He explained that many other neighborhoods had to pay for having streetlights installed. West Savannah could get them free because of added tax bills. This official and Mr. Seckinger had worked out a special grant to get the streetlights installed without cost to anyone, if the community requested them.

"You can get the neighborhood to do anything," the official told me; it being the opinion of Mr. Seckinger.

"Streetlights will cut down on crime," the official told me.

From Friday night until Sunday morning I experienced pure hell. I did not want to ask the church members to sign the petition. I believed it was a compromise to use the church for social improvement. So this predicament baffled me.

I believed the only thing the church should do was to get people saved and to teach the Word of God—not to use its energy to acquire streetlights.

Practicing My Sunday-Morning Rhetoric

I was determined not to announce the streetlight issue on Sunday morning, and not to let the petition be circulated in my church. Nor was I going to allow Mr. Seckinger to personally pass around this petition to the members after the morning service.

I rehearsed the things I would say in the tradition of Elijah, exercising holy boldness as did John Wesley, or preaching as would a fearless frontier preacher.

I kept saying to myself, *Mr. Seckinger, there will be no compromise with bureaucrats; we're not pussy-footin' liberals who want to dangle lights on the corners of our streets.*

Students in my college days were naive and unsuspecting; as a result, guest speakers used absolute terms describing white, absolute white, which was the only thing God liked.

I practiced my rhetoric carefully: *We want to preach Jesus the Light of the world, not get streetlights.*

At the time, I did not realize I had been influenced by a message I had heard at Columbia Bible College. A guest speaker had warned against the insidious creeping liberalism that would strangle the gospel out of our churches.

Students in my college days were naive and unsuspecting; as a result, guest speakers used absolute terms describing white, absolute white, which was the only thing God liked.

As I practiced my rhetoric, I sneered and squinted my eyes as I described black and warned of impending doom should we cross the line into blackness.

The Dangling Streetlights Ridiculed My Faith

On the way to church that Sunday morning, I noticed every streetlight in the city. Of course, the lights were turned off, but because my mind and eyes were focused on streetlights, I saw the innocent streetlights dangling unadorned on light poles.

Eight blocks before I reached Westminster Presbyterian Church, I saw my last streetlight where Augusta Avenue went under the Central of Georgia tracks. Because it was a main intersection, the streetlight was necessary. I passed four streets where African-Americans lived, but they did not have any streetlights. Then approaching my parish, I noticed the four square blocks known as West Savannah did not have streetlights either.

A streetlight is a simple mechanism designed to illuminate where people are walking or driving. That Sunday, however, the lights were menacing instruments, each one laughingly ridiculing my faith. Because I was on my way to church, I should have been singing "My Faith Looks Up to Thee." I could only see red, though. I screwed up my courage, and practiced again my rebuking message to Mr. Seckinger.

A Done Deal

When I arrived at church, I locked my bicycle next to the back door, as usual. As I climbed the brick stairs, I saw Mr. Strickland, also an elder, but he did not ask me to support the petition.

Instead, he assumed it was a done deal because he noted, "When we get these streetlights, more people will come to church on Sunday night, and on Wednesday night."

Mr. Strickland rationalized, "One of the streetlights will be right in front of the church, and the children will probably be playing on the front porch of the church in the evening time; that'll make them more comfortable with the church and they'll come back to Sunday School."

My boldness was only internal. If I were going to argue against it, I should have said something immediately, but Mr. Strickland was older and wiser. I had never won a debate with him so I said nothing.

I had dedicated a point in my sermon under the simple title "Warnings." I would point out how sin gets to us when we compromise with liquor, moving pictures, City Hall and scarlet women. I was then going to add to my denunciation the social gospel and streetlights. I was going to put them all together, then call my people to a rousing defense of the faith.

"Choose you this day whom ye will serve;...as for me and my

house, we will serve the Lord" (Josh. 24:15, *KJV*). I had not preached it yet, but that is what I planned to preach.

"Those streetlights will be nice for the children playing at night," Mrs. Snyder, teacher of the Ladies Bible Class commented as she passed me in the hall.

"That's right," someone else responded.

Everything Was Against Me

I went to my office to pray alone, which was my usual practice before the church service began. Sometimes the room was joyful and sunny and beams of sunlight peered through the stained-glass window. The dark oak paneling of the study hid many stories. Decades of godly men had prayed there; they had interceded for the souls of men and women. I was too young for a study this expensive, so I called it an office. The study, although expensive at one time, had seen better days. I described it as "decayed elegance." The most distinguished Presbyterian pastors had studied there.

Today, however, was different. The stained-glass window was not happy, but the sun struggled to penetrate its darkness. Even the frosted glass in the transom of the door clouded out the hall light. The tall room was more threatening than I remembered, and the light in the ceiling was dimmer.

The large oak desk did not invite me to sit down behind it. A row of bookcases stood along one long wall, each having a glass door to protect the sacred volumes from moisture. One long pew from the back of the auditorium had been placed in front of the glass doors, so I had not made the effort to use the books inside the bookcases. I had removed the old and worn wool carpet, and the naked floor at one time had been brilliantly varnished and polished, but in time had yellowed. Today, the floor pained my knees as I knelt to pray. Everything was against me—the office, the hardwood floor, the elders and the city bureaucrats.

Every time I tried to pray, my request bounced off the tall ceiling. My heart was hollow, and panic echoed in my brain. I did not want to lose, but I could not pray for victory. I could not pray against the streetlights; I could not pray against the elders; I could not pray about anything.

When I tried to review my sermon outlined on 3x5-inch cards, my notes did not sing to me. They were dead.

How can I preach, when I don't feel it? I asked myself.

I heard the pianist play the invocation, which was my signal that it was time for me to open my study door, walk a few feet to the sanctuary and mount the one stair to the pulpit platform. Usually I bounded through the door and floated to the platform. Preaching was my joy. Remember, everybody called me "Preacher."

This morning, however, I did not want to go out the office door. I was afraid of Mr. Seckinger and what he would do. What if I told him no and he made the announcement anyway?

What would the people think? I thought.

I reached for the doorknob, but paused to pray. "Lord, give me boldness to stand for my convictions."

As I entered the auditorium, Mr. Seckinger was standing between me and the pulpit platform.

This is it, I thought as I stopped in front of him. He held the petition in his hand; it was the first time I had seen it. It was nothing but a simple white sheet of paper, and penciled lines indicated where people should sign their names. I could see the typed statement at the top of the worn sheet of paper. Then I saw that the sheet had been signed with several kinds of writing instruments: ink pens, ballpoint pens and hard-lead and soft-lead pencils.

I won't take it if he offers it, I thought, *but what will I say?*

Mr. Seckinger thumped the eraser of a pencil on the paper and announced, "Preacher, we don't need you to make the announcement. Everybody has already signed the petition."

Then he said, grinning widely, "We've got more signatures than we need."

My Main Concern Was My Planned Sermon

It should have been a great relief to me, but it wasn't. It should have meant that I did not have to confront anyone, but I faced another problem. Rather than rejoicing in what had happened, I was immediately terrified with a problem that was much larger to me.

How will I fill five minutes of sermon?

I had planned approximately five minutes of warnings and consequences, but everyone had already signed the petition. Now I had to change my sermon. Rather than being happy or sad, I was frustrated. Here I had planned a pugilistic attack against various evils, but the one that vexed me most was bureaucracy and City Hall, especially its threat to compromise a young soul-winning church. I wanted to keep the first amendment by separating church and state. The congregation had all signed the petition, though, and for all I knew, they may have been signing the petition while I was praying against them—and they probably signed it while sitting in the church pews.

Now my biggest question was, *What am I going to preach?* Not having a great reservoir of knowledge and experience, I planned for

---

Now that I think back on it, perhaps that's why the people liked my preaching. I was loud, enthusiastic and short. Short and to the point.

---

every second of a 20-minute sermon. When I lost a point, I did not have the ability to ad lib. When an illustration was too short, so was my sermon. Now that I think back on it, perhaps that's why the people liked my preaching. I was loud, enthusiastic and short. Short and to the point.

After my confrontation with Mr. Seckinger, I defeatedly mounted the one step to the pulpit platform.

The Petition Made Everyone Happy, Except Me

During the announcements time of the service I said the traditional thing, "Does anybody else have any announcements that need to be made?"

Mr. Seckinger arose and thanked the people for their signatures, telling them they now had more than enough to have the streetlights installed. He was happy, everyone was happy, but the children seemed the happiest.

As the people left church that Sunday morning, two or three chuckled about Mr. Seckinger.

"One of the first nice things he's ever done for the neighborhood," one of the ladies said.

"Thanks, Mr. Seckinger," a young boy waved to him.

The Streetlights Were Right

I pastored the church for another year, never mentioning the streetlights. I never told the people I was against the petition being signed in a church, nor did I ever mention the evil compromise with City Hall.

How could a pastor be against something all his people support?

The answer to that question is simple. The pastor was wrong. He had acquired wrong theology, wrong information and wrong attitudes. He was a simpleton who saw life in two categories: wrong is always black, right is always white. In this case, the streetlights were not black, they were white—as white as light—streetlights were right.

PRINCIPLES TO TAKE AWAY

1. *The principle of obsessive spirituality.* A church's spirituality is not measured in its separation from the world, City Hall or even the "boogie man" that was preached at our theological institutions of training. Rather, spirituality is related to the Holy Spirit who lives through us to manifest the glory of God in the most mundane of situations (e.g., support of a petition to have streetlights installed in the poor area of town). Petitioning for the streetlights was the spiritual thing to do.

2. *The principle of perceived wickedness.* It is sometimes difficult to remember that sin is not a thing, person or even a streetlight or bureaucrat. Sin is an act, attitude or reaction. Sin is the response of the people to the issues of life. As I look back, I realize I perceived that wickedness was found in a simple function of life, and the preacher's response became more wicked than the perceived wickedness of Mr. Seckinger and the bureaucrat.

3. *The principle of the greatest good for the most people.* The propositional gospel of the death, burial and resurrection of Jesus Christ changes our lives when the person of Jesus Christ lives through us to communicate His love to people in the mundane affairs of their lives. Because of my opposition, I lost a great opportunity to be a testimony to the

community. I was never able to capitalize on the congregation's support of streetlights as a testimony of our concern for the community. If I had fought the streetlights as planned, I would have been a barrier to reaching many unsaved and would have created problems in my ministry to the saved.

4. *The principle of protection by reluctance.* If I had immediately responded from the top of my head and the bottom of my heart, I would have alienated my people, the neighborhood and the board of elders. I was quiet, however; they got their streetlights and eventually I saw my error. My youthful reluctance and a withdrawing personality saved me from making many mistakes in my first pastorate that might have otherwise crippled the ministry I had at the time.

"The 'Preacher' traveling by bike and train"

10

"I Saw Jesus"

As a young preacher I had never thought much about seeing Jesus Christ in the flesh. I had heard about the Roman Catholic mystics who had seen Him and touched Him, but I was not sure it had actually happened. I was not sure if anyone could see Jesus, touch Jesus, talk to Jesus—that is, the actual, physical Jesus who had walked in the flesh and had been crucified on the cross.

No textbook is available to help a young preacher with his first congregation. He encounters many strange and wonderful experiences, and he will meet people who claim to have seen and talked with Jesus.

An Unusual Encounter

Of all the men in the church, I trusted Mr. Miller. I had visited his house when he was drunk, and preached the sermon when he walked forward in church and was born again. I saw his life turn around; he became a new creature in Jesus Christ.

The Bible says, "Behold, all things have become new" (2 Cor. 5:17).

Mr. Miller carried his Bible to church, asked significant questions of me and even went visiting with me, soul winning door-to-door in the neighborhood. He was truly changed from darkness to light. So when he told me he saw and talked with Jesus, I could not doubt the source. I could not accuse him of being emotionally unfit or a busybody wanting a reputation or wanting to stir up trouble. Mr. Miller was solid.

One Sunday afternoon I was in my office at the church, preparing a sermon for that night. I heard a knock at the door and saw that it was Mr. Miller.

"I got something important to talk with you about..." Mr. Miller let the words trail off into nothing.

He was a straightforward man, and was responsible for several people who worked for him at the Central of Georgia Railway. He did not stutter, but there he sat in my office running the rim of his hat around in circles, staring at the floor.

Miller was a grizzly man; even when well shaven he looked as if he needed a shave. Black chest hair stood out over his white shirt next to the Adam's apple.

Miller continued to fumble over the words, then finally blurted it out.

"Jesus came and stood at the foot of my bed this morning..." that was it, he did not finish his sentence. He just told me Jesus came into his room and stood at the foot of his bed.

My first response was unbelief. I did not really believe Jesus had been in West Savannah, nor did I believe he had been in Mr. Miller's house, but what was I going to say? I did not want to call him a liar. I did not even want to question his credibility. I did not know what to say; I quickly and silently prayed for Jesus to help me know what to say.

"Did he talk to you?" I asked.

I did not immediately ask what Jesus looked like; I did that later in the conversation. My first question was to know the words Jesus might have said.

"Jesus said he wanted my car," Mr. Miller said.

That news also bothered me. I figured that if Jesus were on earth,

He would walk, or could instantly transpose Himself from one site to another. Never in my wildest thoughts had I ever thought Jesus would want a car.

So I repeated the words, "Jesus wants your car?" I lifted my voice at the end of the sentence to make it sound like a question.

"Yep."

The conversation was cut off for a couple of seconds. Mr. Miller did not say anything nor did he look up at me. I was trying to register in my mind what I was hearing and not trying to interpret it.

All I could say was, "Hum-m-m-m-m-m-m-m."

Again the room was silent. The warm sun from the west streamed in on the yellow walls and a housefly buzzed on the warm window pane, trying to get outside. The bumping of the fly on the window pane was the only noise in the room. Then Mr. Miller started relating the whole story.

The Jesus Encounter

"Jesus told me that if He came to Bull and Broad Street (the geographical center of Savannah, Georgia) and announced to the city that He needed a car, no one could get within two or three miles of

---

Mr. Miller continued about what Jesus had said: "'I want you to give your car to the preacher every weekend.'"

---

the intersection. If everybody saw Him or heard Him announce from the tallest building that He needed a car, everyone would create the biggest traffic jam this city has ever seen to give their cars to Him."

I was amazed that Jesus knew the geographical boundaries of Savannah, Georgia, but what Mr. Miller said made sense to me.

Mr. Miller continued about what Jesus had said: "'I want you to give your car to the preacher every weekend.'"

I knew exactly what he was saying because everyone called me

"Preacher" and I knew he was telling me Jesus wanted him to give me his car.

"Understand me," Miller quickly clarified, "not give you my car for keeps, but let you use my car each weekend."

Back in the '50s, clergymen received passes to ride in the coach of any railway train at almost giveaway prices. I could ride from Columbia, South Carolina, to Savannah, Georgia, for 53 cents. I did not travel on the Central of Georgia Railway where Mr. Miller worked, though, but on the Southern Railway, which also used Central of Georgia terminal.

My routine was to take the train from Columbia, South Carolina, to Savannah, Georgia, leave the terminal and board the bus at West Broad Street and Augusta Road, drop my eight-cent token into the slot and ride the bus to the church.

The hospitals were approximately eight miles away, and I used my English racing bike to make my hospital visits. I was a little embarrassed that I was not as sophisticated as were the other ministers in Savannah. I always parked my racing bike in the back of the hospital and locked it to a gas meter, then rolled down my pant leg, adjusted my suit coat and walked with dignity up the front stairs to make my pastoral calls.

I did not have a car, the freedom of a car, nor access to a car. I never even thought about wanting a car or purchasing a car. I was accomplishing the commuting job on a bicycle and the city bus.

Receiving Detailed Instructions

Mr. Miller continued to tell me what Jesus told him to do. "When you come into town on the Southern Railway, don't get off the train and walk into the terminal."

Then Mr. Miller instructed me, "Rather, turn and walk out into the railway yard where my office is."

Mr. Miller's office was located in a little shack about 10 feet square in the middle of the railway yard. He was the yard pilot; he guided trains in and out the Central of Georgia Railway station. His was a crucial job because the Central of Georgia required every train to back into the station, and his job was to help the trains back in. His job was similar to the person who helps a semi-truck driver back into a parking stall.

He continued, "I'll leave my Ford parked right next to my office shack." Then he explained, "The key will be in the ignition; take the car and use it all weekend. The tank will be full of gas."

"But someone will steal it..." I began to reason and tell him it was not a good idea.

"If Jesus told me to leave the car there for you, He'll make sure no one steals it," Mr. Miller explained.

Then he told me that when I finished my church duties on Sunday evening, I should drive his car back to the station, leave his car parked by the shack and he would get it the next morning after he rode the bus to work. Again, I wanted to remind him that leaving his car in that neighborhood overnight was risky. I wanted to tell him someone would steal it. He immediately knew what was on my mind.

"Nobody will steal it, because we're doing what Jesus wants," Mr. Miller said.

I asked him, "Are you sure it was Jesus, and not an angel?"

"I ought to know who Jesus is; after all, He saved me," Miller replied to me.

I did not want to take the man's brand-new Ford—this was 1953 and he drove a dark blue 1952 four-door Ford. I would be driving one of the fanciest cars of any minister in Savannah, Georgia. I did not think I was worthy of the Ford, and I was not sure I could take it. I began to think of how I could turn down the car offer.

Miller must have known what was going on in my mind because he said, "I am not giving this car to you, I am loaning it to Jesus."

Seeing Jesus Was a Sure Thing

After Mr. Miller told me what Jesus had told him to do about the car, I got around to asking him what Jesus looked like. Miller told me Jesus had blond hair, a blond beard and a kind face.

"Did he shine?" I continued to ask him, not a skeptical question, but rather a curious one.

"Just a little bit."

"What do you mean a little bit?" I asked.

"He wasn't so bright that He hurt my eyes like looking into a spotlight," Mr. Miller said. "He had a little shine like the exit light in the movies."

I understood what he was saying, but I was not sure he had actually seen Jesus.

So I asked him, "Are you sure it was Jesus, and not an angel?" I gave him an opportunity to back away from his story.

"I ought to know who Jesus is; after all, He saved me," Miller replied to me. He was using all the integrity of a shivering, cold, wet person who is telling you the water is freezing in the pool.

I did not question him any further because he might think I did not believe he saw Jesus. At the time I was not really sure he had seen Jesus. My theology told me that any appearance of Jesus was a post-Resurrection appearance, and He had not done that since He returned to heaven at the Ascension. So theologically I did not believe Mr. Miller had really seen Jesus. At least that is what my head told me, but I was not sure in my heart.

A Gift of Commitment

So every week after that encounter I took Mr. Miller's car from the railway yard and drove it to win souls. I was able to drive farther, do more and do it more quickly. This stretched my weekends, hence packing more into my weekends than I would have been able to do without a car. As a result, I won more people to Christ than I would have done otherwise.

As I look back on the experience, do I now think Mr. Miller saw Jesus? I do not know the answer, but I do know we would not have accomplished what God did in West Savannah without the car. Not only did it economize my time, but it also laid a heavier burden on me to the commitment of soul winning.

Savannah is known for its gully washers when the bottom drops out of the sky and all the water in the world comes down. Mr. Miller never once backed away from this commitment in more than a year. He rode the bus to work in the rain, and ran through the muddy parking lot to his shack in the middle of the Central of Georgia Railway yard. He did all this without a complaint, without a second thought, without a doubt—because he had seen Jesus.

When I realized that Mr. Miller was riding the bus in the cold and the rain, I never once misused his car. I was conscientious to make as many evangelistic calls as I possibly could, knowing that is what Jesus would tell me to do if He came and stood at the foot of my bed.

Principles to Take Away

1. *The tub principle.* I often say that each tub sits on its own bottom, and each person is responsible for his or her actions and words to God. Whether I completely believed Mr. Miller had actually seen the physical Jesus in the flesh is not the issue. The issue is that he was completely obedient to what he perceived to be the command of Jesus to him about his car. Because Mr. Miller was completely obedient, whether I agreed or not, I followed through with the same instructions and was true in my integrity to his gift of commitment.

2. *The can-do principle.* Who am I to tell God what He can do or what He cannot do? Do I have the right to say that Jesus cannot actually reveal Himself in the flesh in West Savannah, Georgia? I may think Jesus will not reveal Himself in the flesh, but that is only an opinion. I am careful not to tell people what God will or will not do, because God can do anything He wants to do, and will do anything He wants to do.

3. *The provoke principle.* The dedication and good works of one person will provoke another to better service of Jesus Christ. Miller's gift of a car to me did something he was unable to do. He was not a soul winner, and to my knowledge did not actually lead anyone to Jesus Christ while I was his pastor. I, however, probably led someone to Christ every week in West Savannah as a result of using his car to economize my time and energy. Although I may be the actual tool God used, as much credit goes to Miller as to any other human vehicle.

"My 'shoot-out' at OK Corral"

11

Whose Church Is It Anyway?

Every young pastor has a "shoot-out" with the official board. Somewhere along the line, a young pastor has been questioned, called down, voted down or had his wings clipped. My "shoot-out" at OK Corral came approximately three to four months after I became the pastor of Westminster Presbyterian Church.

My World Crashed Inward

On the inevitable Saturday afternoon, the sun was pouring through the stained-glass window in my office; my mood was happy, and I was preparing my Sunday sermon. I had just spent two hours knocking on doors and talking to people about Jesus Christ. I was expecting a great day on Sunday, and was writing some notes on 3x5-inch cards for my sermon the following day.

I heard scratching at the front door of the church. Next I heard steps coming down the hallway to my office. Through the large milk-glass panel of the office door between my office and the hallway I could see two bodily forms standing in the hallway.

"Come on in!" I shouted.

At the door stood Mr. Seckinger and Mr. Strickland, two men who attended the church. They had started attending the worship service after the five women who had the key to the front door "called" me to be their pastor. Neither Mr. Seckinger nor Mr. Strickland was married to any of the five ladies who had called me to be their pastor. Neither of the men had been saved during my ministry. Both Seckinger and Strickland were members of the church before it was disbanded by Independent Presbyterian Church.

The two men announced to me, "We are elders."

Upon hearing that statement my world crashed inward. I had never thought about elders, deacons or any kind of board. I had never asked anyone in the community if the church had an elder or deacon board before it closed its doors. I had never tried to find the old membership list before the church shut its doors. I was not interested in history; I was only interested in the *now*, and the future.

Disapproval of My Pastoring

"We don't approve the way things are going..." elderly Seckinger let the words die in the middle of the room. Then he said nothing.

I usually react in one of two ways to criticism. Sometimes I have a knee-jerk reaction, as though kicking a dog off the porch. Because I have a timid side, I apologize or run away. At other times I get mad when someone criticizes me. I raise the fur on my back and go into an attack mode.

When I heard the phrase, "We don't approve the way things are going...," my world collapsed.

No one in the church had criticized me. I thought everyone liked my preaching. When people left the service, they shook my hands and told me what a good preacher I was. I believed them. Almost every Sunday somebody walked forward to the altar to be saved. I thought that was God's approval on my actions.

"We don't approve of the way things are going..." Seckinger

broke the silence and again left the words dangling in the room for more silence.

I was stunned at the two men's attack. They had attended the church and had heard me preach. I had been in both their homes three or four times. I could not think of any reason they would not approve of what I was doing.

"We're gonna have an elders' meeting right now..." again the elderly Seckinger spit out the words and let them die in midair.

I began to shake.

I don't know if my shaking was out of fear because these men were elders, and as a Presbyterian I knew the elders controlled the church.

Perhaps my shaking was because of anger. They had let the old church die. They had let Independent Presbyterian Church close the doors. They were responsible for the death of the church and I was responsible for its resurrection, for its new life, for the salvation of more than 50 people.

My First Unexpected Elders' Meeting

Mr. Seckinger called the meeting to order, and then assumed the position of moderator of the elders. He announced that was the position he held before the church was shut down. Mr. Seckinger appointed Mr. Strickland as secretary. I don't know if they recognized me as an elder or as their pastor. I don't know if they recognized me at all. At least they did not ask me to leave. Then came the first item of business.

Attacking My Authority to Paint the Church

"Why didn't you ask us for permission to paint the church?" Seckinger inquired.

Mr. Strickland chimed in, "Yeah, we've been discussing that; why didn't you ask us?"

It dawned on me they had been discussing this item among themselves, and now I was on the spot. My voice became high and tight.

I squeaked, "You knew about it," I protested to Mr. Seckinger, "you even brought a ladder for painting the church."

Then turning to Mr. Strickland, I said, "You even got a donation of paint for the church, and helped organize the equipment."

"Yes," Seckinger's scowling face revealed anger, "but you didn't ask us before you announced it to the church."

Nowhere in my youthful thinking did I ever imagine I needed permission to paint a church. The building needed paint, so I just got it done. The boards were rotten, the paint was peeling; the building was falling apart.

"I decided it needed to be painted, and I thought it was God's will," I told the men. "Since the Lord wanted it to be painted, I told the people and when they agreed, I thought that was all the permission I needed."

They knew my answer ahead of time, but just did not like it. Then came the next question.

Questioning the Money Issue

"Where's all the money going?" Seckinger's inquisition continued.

"Mrs. Silla Hair has the money," I explained.

"What have you done with the money?"

"I've never touched any of the money, I don't even count it."

"Who gave Mrs. Hair the authority to keep the church's money?"

I again went into a long explanation of how the church was reconstituted. I explained to them how the ladies had the key to the building, and began teaching Sunday School. They later invited me to come and preach, and they collected money among themselves to pay for my train ticket back to Columbia, South Carolina.

Explaining the Authority of the Presbytery

Then I told Mr. Seckinger and Mr. Strickland about the two pastors who came to the church one Saturday afternoon to find out why I had opened the Westminster Presbyterian Church. Then it dawned on me: I was a man under authority, but not their authority.

So I blurted out, "I am under the authority of Reverend Carroll Stegall, pastor of Eastern Heights Presbyterian Church."

I explained to the two men that the Presbytery had reconstituted the church and placed me under Rev. Stegall's supervision, my home pastor.

The List of Dislikes

Seckinger and Strickland presented a list of five or six other things they did not like.

They did not like the potted plants around the pulpit.

They did not like the loud rhythmic way I rang the bell at 9:00 A.M. every Sunday morning.

They did not like my visiting every house in the neighborhood because some of the neighbors belonged to the Salvation Army, the Pentecostal church and a Baptist church on Highway 17.

They accused me of leaving out "Presbyterian things" from the worship service, such as repeating the Apostles' Creed and reading from both the Old Testament and New Testament.

On this last point they were right. I only read the Scriptures based on the sermon I preached; sometimes from the Old Testament, sometimes from the New.

They did not like people visiting the church and parking on the front grass. During a rainstorm some of the people had driven right across the grass and let people out of the car at the front steps, leaving ruts in the grass.

Mr. Seckinger said, "We're not poor white trash that leaves cars all over the yard."

He was angry at some of the people who had been saved in the church.

"Make them keep their cars off the grass," Seckinger barked.

The List of Demands

Seckinger told me they wanted me to do several things from now on. He pulled a tablet sheet out of his pocket, and several more items were written down in pencil, all needing their permission.

1. Get permission to spend any money.
2. Get permission for any special meetings that are not a part of the general schedule.
3. Get permission for any special speakers or special music.
4. Get permission for anyone who will fill the pulpit if the preacher is not there.

I looked at the list of demands. All my freedom to lead the church was taken from me. As the pastor, I believed God led me to bring in special music or to have a friend from Bible college come and speak to the young people. God had blessed my plans, not their plans.

I was being handcuffed.

When Mr. Seckinger closed the meeting in prayer, the two men rose and walked out of the office. I thought they might have thanked me for reopening the church, being instrumental in people being saved or doing a good job.

Coming to Terms

The sunshine through the stained-glass window dried up. The air was heavy, and my delightful office that gave me so much happiness, and a sense of power, suddenly was threatening. The yellow paint was dirty, the curtains were grungy, the oak panels were old and scarred. The presence of God seemed to leave the office. It was Ichabod (i.e., no glory).

I cried in my office for a long while. I was 20 years old and it had been a long time since I had shed tears. Tears dripped onto my oak desk and spattered my sermon notes.

Somewhere a still small voice whispered to me,

"Don't use the pulpit to attack individuals;

don't use the pulpit for pettiness."

I bounced alternatively between anger and retreat.

The first thing I decided was, *Tomorrow I will resign, go back to Columbia Bible College and let them keep their church.*

I thought better of that. The two former elders had not called me to be the pastor, and they were not going to run me off. I decided to fight. I began writing a sermon and decided to answer each of the accusations. I was going to read them and answer them. I was going to attack Seckinger and Strickland, face-to-face, from the pulpit.

I am going to scorch them tomorrow, I decided.

I took the seven points of criticism, and began to put together a sermon describing what God had done in the church. I was going to describe to the congregation the furor and criticisms of Seckinger and Strickland. Then I was going to answer them.

I knelt in prayer and offered my petitions to God, but my prayers bounced off the ceiling. God began crushing my spirit. I felt righteous indignation, but my prayers would not let me preach in the pulpit what I wanted to preach.

Somewhere a still small voice whispered to me, *Don't use the pulpit to attack individuals; don't use the pulpit for pettiness.*

After praying, God answered my prayer, but God did it differently from what I had prayed.

I was praying for God to remove them, to change their minds—just for God to do my thing. God's answer was to remind me of Rev. Stegall, my counselor.

Wise Counsel from My Supervisor

I decided to phone Rev. Carroll Stegall, but Westminster Presbyterian Church did not have a phone installed on the premises. I thought about going to one of the neighbors to make my phone call, but I did not want anyone to hear my problem. I was embarrassed. So I got on my racing bike and rode two miles to the Central of Georgia Railway station.

Finding a phone booth and putting a nickel into the slot, I phoned Rev. Stegall. As soon as he picked up the receiver, I blurted out my problem. I am sure he heard my anger, or frustration.

Then he began to laugh in cadence. "Ho-ho, ho-ho, ho-ho," the barrel-chested Stegall laughed into the phone heartily.

I did not think it was funny, though.

"You are going through what every young preacher faces," the wise Stegall began to counsel me and prepared me for the inevitable.

"First," Stegall pointed me to Presbyterian law, "when a Presbyterian church is reduced into mission status, or voted out of existence, the offices of elders and deacons are eliminated."

"What's that?" I said to myself.

"Seckinger and Strickland are not elders," the laughing Stegall told me.

The sun came out, the day became brighter. My countenance began to lift. Stegall told me that Seckinger and Strickland were no longer elders in the church until they were voted back into office by the Presbytery. Stegall assured me that although Seckinger and Strickland had been elders, and they understood what elders did, they no longer had any legal authority at Westminster Presbyterian Church.

Stegall warned me, however, "They are elderly men, wise men, powerful men."

He told me I would have to handle the men very carefully

because many in the community respected them. The Savannah Presbytery also respected them because they had once been office holders in the church. Stegall reminded me that if these men called someone in the Presbytery to complain about me, although they could not fire me, they could get me fired; or at least they could cause a lot of trouble for me.

Then Stegall asked me, "Who's got the checkbook?"

I explained to him that Mrs. Silla Hair had the checkbook. I explained that the money was counted each week by three or four people, deposited into the Citizens and Southern National Bank and the bills were paid out of the money.

[Stegall] reminded me of the Golden Rule,

"He who has the gold, rules."

Stegall then asked me two more questions.

"Are you happy with the way the ladies are taking care of the money?"

"Yes."

"Will the ladies spend the money the way you want it spent?"

"Yes."

Then Stegall told me not to worry about anything. The person who controlled the money had the authority in the church.

He reminded me of the Golden Rule, "He who has the gold, rules."

Then Stegall gave me some wise counsel about how to handle Seckinger and Strickland.

"Call them into the office every Sunday morning before you preach. Tell them everything you are doing. Give them your plans before you announce anything to the church."

Stegall told me to respect them and call on them to pray.

Then he instructed me, "You tell those men that according to Presbyterian law they are not elders, but you want their permission to call them elders and to recognize them as elders in public."

Stegall explained to me that I should honor them by using the title "elder." He warned me very carefully, however, "Never let them vote on anything. You must not ask them to vote on any of your projects because that would give them authority."

He told me to make sure a full public account was made of every check spent by the church, and every penny that came into the account was accurately posted. He told me to make sure three people always counted the offering, and I should never touch any money. I should never sign a check. I should never carry the money to the treasurer even if she were not in a church service.

"If you touch the money once," Stegall warned, "they will scalp you."

Respecting My Elders

Sunday morning—the following day—before church I asked Mr. Seckinger and Mr. Strickland to meet me in my office for prayer. I then announced to them what Mr. Stegall had said: they were no longer elders, but I asked them if I might publicly call them elders. I asked them for their wisdom to help guide the church.

"We never heard that before," Mr. Seckinger said to me. He was talking about the fact that elders lose their appointment when a church is reduced to mission status or voted out of existence.

Mr. Seckinger and Mr. Strickland never told me if I could publicly call them "elders."

They never called an elders' meeting during the following year.

I, however, publicly called them "elders," and each Sunday morning they met with me for prayer before the church service began.

I discussed all the church plans with them, but I also invited Mr. Miller to be present in the room with us.

I began repeating the Apostles' Creed and read from both the Old and New Testament in church, as Mr. Seckinger had suggested. From time to time Mr. Seckinger would suggest things we could all do in the church, and to the best of my knowledge I always followed his suggestions.

After our confrontation and the first elders' meeting, we developed a good relationship. Mr. Seckinger and Mr. Strickland never told me whether they ever contacted another minister in the Savannah Presbytery concerning their official status. I think they probably might have because they lived by the rules Rev. Carroll Stegall gave me.

PRINCIPLES TO TAKE AWAY

1. *The principle of the crushed rose.* Young preachers are like a rose that desires to give fragrance and beauty to other people. Church officials should realize that when they destroy the confidence and optimism of the minister, they are crushing the fragrance of God's blessing to their lives and the lives of others.

2. *The principle of good information.* Too often we get mad or we quit because someone has given us bad information. The principle is simply this: We make good decisions on good information, bad decisions on bad information, and if we don't have any information, we make lucky decisions. Some of our lucky decisions work out for good, and some of our lucky decisions work out for our harm. Before reacting to criticism about your ministry, make sure you have full information about the attack and your attackers.

3. *The principle of the iron fist with the velvet glove.* Stegall told me to be firm with Seckinger and Strickland, not to let them control the church nor me. That was the iron fist. He told me to be kind, respectful and to use them wherever I could. That was the velvet glove.

4. *The principle of incredulous absurdity.* Stegall laughed at me when I told him about the proposed elders' meetings and what I was supposed to do. He had not given the two men any credibility because he knew they had no authority. The absurdity with which he treated them was equal to the absurdity by which they treated me. I learned an important principle from Rev. Stegall: Sometimes it is better to laugh than to get mad. Your anger always makes you lose, while laughter makes you infectious.

"The eager 'Westerners'"

12

No One Came to Vacation Bible School

I sat dejectedly on the stage next to the pulpit. The five ladies who had called me to the church sat on the front pew of the auditorium and listened with funeral dread.

No one had come to Vacation Bible School—not one visitor.

My world collapsed on me and I was paralyzed. I was on the verge of tears and the ladies could see "defeat" written in every word I said and every time I shifted my sitting position.

Failure.

Not only had I failed my first outreach event, but I was also about to cry in front of the ladies and convince them I was only an immature 20-year-old boy.

Although I never had trouble persuading people to come and hear me preach, I did not understand the dynamics of marketing and advertising to attract a crowd for other outreach events. The people of West Savannah came to hear me preach because I went door-to-door to invite them to church.

I had been in every home in our neighborhood many times. Because only 40 to 50 houses were located in the neighborhood, it was easy to saturate my Jerusalem. I had gone door-to-door, asking people if they were born again, reading John 3 to them, reminding them Jesus told Nicodemus, "Ye must be born again" (v. 7, *KJV*). That concern, however, was not translated into Vacation Bible School (VBS).

Planning a Western Vacation Bible School

In the summer of 1953, I planned and led my first Vacation Bible School. For those not familiar with this church program, a Vacation Bible School is conducted each morning during the summer at the church from approximately 9:00 A.M. until noon for a one- or two-week time period. Here children are taught the Word of God, play games and experience various other Christian activities to involve them in learning the faith. Because children are having a summer vacation from school, many parents have seen Vacation Bible School as a built-in "baby-sitter," hence many unchurched children are reached for Christ.

I had not thought about planning a Vacation Bible School, but one day the five ladies who had called me to the church gathered around me after one of my sermons and talked about Vacation Bible School.

"We need to start planning early," Mrs. Miller exhorted me.

After a planning session and agreeing to sponsor VBS that summer, I went to Swanebeck's Bible and Book Store to look at available teaching materials. I purchased a VBS planning kit, and resolved to follow the preplanning steps meticulously. The five ladies who were planning the VBS along with me were my teachers, so gathering a staff was no problem. We scheduled two training sessions, and each of them went according to plan.

We planned a Western theme, so on Sunday afternoon after my morning sermon—the day before VBS was to begin—the ladies and I hauled some lumber into the sanctuary and constructed a corral in front of the piano. Mrs. Smith constructed a large red barn in the back of the pulpit from several packets of red construction paper.

Straw was thrown all over the platform in front of the pulpit to resemble the floor of a barn.

Because I was teaching junior boys, I hung some cap pistols and holsters on my classroom wall. Under them was displayed a "Red Rider" BB gun. I had borrowed these items from Richard, my little brother.

Each teacher carefully lettered the Bible memory verses on cards and attached them to the sanctuary walls.

The Big Day Arrived

Early Monday morning of the first day of Bible School, the five ladies and I came to the church around 6:00 A.M. to build four corrals in the front yard of the church. Our plans were to "corral" the children into these pens, then march into the sanctuary for Vacation Bible School while singing a Christian chorus. I dug holes in the front lawn for the logs that became the corner posts. Bringing in split rails would have been too difficult, so we stretched crepe-paper "logs" from corner pole to corner pole and made four corrals— kindergarten, beginner, primary and junior. A large sign printed on paper laundry bags identified each corral.

Then from one pillar on the front porch to the other, we hung a large banner under which the children and teachers would march into church, supposedly singing a Christian chorus. We had purchased the banner displaying a Western motto from the Christian supplier of VBS material.

The staff was dressed in Western clothing. The teenage boys and I wore blue jeans, flannel shirts and boots, and had tied kerchiefs around our necks. Two of the women draped children's cowboy hats over the back of their necks, the way we thought cowboys did.

We expected a hundred children for Vacation Bible School, so Mrs. Silla Hair set out a hundred paper cups on tables in the church kitchen to fill with Kool-Aid at snack time. Not wanting to be stingy, we had put more than 500 cookies on plates, ready for hungry little Westerners.

Waiting for the "Westerners" to Arrive
At about five minutes to eight, I walked out to the front porch to count the children, and to my surprise only five or six children were standing in the corrals, and they were not behaving. These were the

children of the five ladies who were my VBS teachers.

"Hey, kids," I yelled, "don't tear that crepe paper down!"

I wanted the crepe-paper logs to remain intact for the visual effect. I wanted all the children to feel the Western theme.

I went back inside the church and asked Mrs. Hair, "Where are all the children?"

"They'll be along."

H-m-m-m, I thought.

"About 40 of them came last year," Mrs. Hair responded.

At eight o'clock I went back out to the front yard—still only five or six children were playing and by this time none of them were inside the corrals.

"Get back into the corrals!" I yelled. "We're almost ready to begin."

I am an early person, so I like to be early for every event because I don't like to waste other people's time. I have always thought there are only two kinds of people in the world—early people and late people. No one ever comes on time. Those who think they come on time, don't; they are usually a minute or two late. So I wanted to start Vacation Bible School on time, but only five or six children were there.

"Let's wait 5 or 10 minutes," Mrs. Silla Hair said to me.

Everything was prepared—all the decorations were in place, the food was ready and the corrals were set up, so we sat at the front of the church sanctuary waiting. I sat on the platform next to the pulpit, and the ladies sat in the first pew. The longer I sat there, the more the ladies could read my face. I was getting more discouraged by the minute.

Every two minutes I nervously jumped up, walked to the back door of the sanctuary, counted children again and repeated to the ladies, "Still only five or six children."

By 8:20 I was devastated. I symbolically sat in front of the ladies, as a pastor should as a leader for his people, but I was slipping beyond despondency to despair.

No one has come.

Sure, more than 10 people were at the church, but the 10 people represented 5 ladies, their children and the pastor.

"They'll come," Mrs. Miller kept saying, "let's just be patient, they came last year."

At 8:45 each of the ladies could see on my face the feelings of my heart. My enthusiasm was drained, my spirit was gone and my smile had disappeared. This was the first Vacation Bible School I

My enthusiasm was drained, my spirit was gone and my smile had disappeared. Of all the events I had planned for Westminster Presbyterian Church, this was the biggest. Yet it could only be described in one word: failure.

---

had ever planned. Of all the events I had planned for Westminster Presbyterian Church, this was the biggest.

Yet it could only be described in one word: *failure.*

My mind closed in on me and I could not think. I wanted to keep up my optimism in front of the ladies, but how could I? I did not have a clue what to do next. I had believed God would bless the Vacation Bible School. We had held two special cottage prayer meetings, praying specifically for Vacation Bible School. We had prayed that children might get saved and that we might reach their parents for Christ.

We could not have done more to plan the Vacation Bible School, decorate for the Vacation Bible School, pray for the Vacation Bible School—we could not have done more.

My nervousness began to freeze over; I no longer jumped up and ran to the door to count the children. I sat paralyzed by failure; I could not move.

Therefore, when I came to the place where I did not know what to do, I resorted back to a familiar line, "We ought to spend some time in prayer."

"We've already done that," Mrs. Silla Hair overruled my suggestion.

"Let's go get the children," Mrs. Hair then said.

An Inviting Parade

Mrs. Hair suggested having a Vacation Bible School parade, which seemed like a good idea—we had nothing to lose at that point. We would decorate the five cars and cruise the neighborhood to invite children to VBS.

"We'll start VBS at 10:00," Mrs. Hair announced.

So we got out the balloons and Scotch Tape. All of us blew a lot of hot air into the balloons, then we began decorating five cars in front of the church. We took our banner from the pillars at the front door and draped it across the radiator of the first car. Then this noisy crew in tacky-looking cars began honking horns, yelling and waving at everyone, slowly going down Fourth Avenue.

While we were driving, the children delivered handbills. They ran from house to house and put the handbills on the front doors of every house in the neighborhood. We invited everyone in sight to come to Vacation Bible School. We made enough noise to wake up the neighborhood and invite every child to attend Vacation Bible School.

It worked.

I was yelling at the top of my voice, "We're starting at 10:00 A.M.!"

I pointed back to the church and added, "Make sure your children are there."

Ladies came to their doors, we yelled and waved at them, and the ladies waved back. Silla Hair or one of the ladies in the cars knew most of them by name, and they explained to them what they were doing. Some of the men in the neighborhood, however, worked night shifts on one of the railway lines, so they were not pleased to be awakened by honking horns, yelling VBS leaders and laughing children.

One man came to the front door wearing only an undershirt and shorts, pumped his fist in the air and yelled, "Shut your d____ mouths!"

"We'll be gone in a minute!" Silla Hair smilingly yelled back.

Let Vacation Bible School Begin

That morning about 40 children came to Vacation Bible School. The corrals were gone by the time they arrived. Instead of waiting in the front yard as we had planned, children just meandered into the sanctuary because Mrs. Smith was playing the piano by that time.

The following day we planned starting time for 9:00 A.M. because 8:00 A.M. was too early for most of the people in the neighborhood.

That week we had a contest for each child to bring a friend, and it worked. By the end of the week almost 100 children attended Vacation Bible School. I don't remember the average attendance, nor

---

I remember learning my lesson about targeting the right audience by using promotion, advertising and action: "Let's go get the children."

---

do I remember how many children came to know Jesus Christ.

Overall we did think, however, that the VBS had been a success, although off to a slow—extremely slow—start.

Learning from Hindsight

I do remember learning my lesson about targeting the right audience by using promotion, advertising and action: "Let's go get the children."

I had planned the Vacation Bible School flawlessly. We had held prayer meetings and teacher training meetings, had planned the decorations—everything was ready. The only problem was that I never adequately planned an advertising and outreach campaign in the community.

Although I had promoted the forthcoming VBS during church announcements, children did not come to the Vacation Bible School because they did not know we were sponsoring a Bible School. Most of the children went home after Sunday School, thus did not hear the VBS announcements in the morning worship services. Had I put up the decorations before Sunday School the day before we started VBS, it would have generated excitement, but I didn't. We waited till Sunday afternoon to decorate, so many people did not pay attention to our attempts at promoting VBS.

Using Proper Promotion Techniques

One month later I planned an evangelistic crusade in the church, and I had learned my lesson from opening-day failure of Vacation Bible School. Because I used a proper promotion campaign, the evangelistic meeting was a success.

I targeted the right audience by using promotion, advertising and action: "Let's go get the people."

When the people *knew* about the meetings, they came.

When the people *felt* they had a reason to attend the meetings, they came.

When the people *decided* they wanted to attend the meetings, they came.

In my promotion, I appealed to people's intellect, emotion and wisdom. I made use of the laws of communication by marketing and advertising to motivate people to attend our church meetings. That, among other things, made all the difference in conducting a successful meeting.

PRINCIPLES TO TAKE AWAY

1. *The principle of the law of communication.* When we pray for God to do things, we should be careful not to ask Him to break the laws by which he runs the universe. Just as it is impossible to communicate from a vacuum, so we should not expect people in our community to attend church services if they don't know about the church services. Can we ask God to send people to a church service they don't know about? People are made in the image of God, which means they have intellect, emotion and will (i.e., they have personality). Therefore, they must *know* about church meetings, *feel* a reason to attend church meetings and they must *decide* to attend church meetings. Rather than asking God to violate the laws of communication, or transcend the laws of communication, we should make use of the laws of communication by marketing and advertising to motivate people to attend our church meetings.

2. *The principle of the law of division of labor.* The work of God is divided into two equal distinct spheres: the work of God and the work of humans. God convicts of sin, reveals His Word to blinded minds and motivates people to be converted (i.e., God works internally in the hearts of people). On the other side of the door, God expects us to go to the people, as He has commanded. God expects us to gather the people, as He has commanded. God expects us to work so "my house may be filled" (Luke 14:23). When we do our work best, God is able to do His work best and effectively. God will not do for us what He has commanded us to do, and we cannot do what God has reserved as His sphere of influence.

3. *The principle of the law of prepared communication.* Whereas I had prepared for Vacation Bible School by planning cottage prayer meetings, teacher training, advertising and covered every organizational detail, I had not communicated the outreach event to the community. We should learn that we cannot do the work of God with mere organization and preparation within the church house; we must also prepare communication and advertising within the targeted area. We can't do the work of God with *just* communication and advertising, but we probably won't do the work of God without advertising and communication.

4. *The principle of balanced outreach.* Consider the two facets in church growth. The first aspect is internal growth, which involves spiritual factors, things such as prayer, revival and the working of the spirit of God in people's hearts. The second aspect is external growth, which involves the natural factors such as inviting friends, advertising and getting people to be committed to attend church services. Some churches go from one extreme to another, but those that have a balanced outreach are those that are most effective.

5. *The principle of leadership reinforcement.* When I as a leader had done all I could to encourage children to attend Vacation Bible School, I was discouraged and gave up because no one came. One of those I was leading reinforced my leadership by suggesting something very sim-

ple: "Let's go get the children." When I could not think of one thing to snatch Vacation Bible School from the jaws of failure, the most obvious answer was, "We need children." The only thing to do was to go get them.

6. *The principle of the obvious.* Sometimes leaders don't know what to do when they are boxed in and feel defeated. Rather than looking inward for the causes of failure, or giving up in frustration, leaders ought to do what is most obvious. Most churches have an empty-pew problem. Not enough people are attending to listen to sermons or Bible lessons. The most obvious answer is: "Let's go get the people." Many pastors think they are failures because people don't come to hear them preach, even though they prepare well, plan well and pray sufficiently. The most obvious answer to their problem is: "Let's go get the people."

"Earl McQuay conducted a successful revival meeting"

13

It Takes Only One

On July 7, 1953, an old-fashioned "atmospheric" revival at Westminster Presbyterian Church began, in which the Lord "poured His Spirit" on the people. A total of 37 adults were converted and many children made public professions of faith. Brothers who argued for years came to the altar to embrace in reconciliation. People went to the neighborhood store to pay off bills they owed. The altar was filled with sobbing people, people hungry for the touch of God, people confessing secret sins.

Preparing a Sermon to Promote Revival

One of the keys to the success of the crusade was the sermon I preached the Sunday before the crusade began. I thought it was a "poor" sermon producing "poor" results because only one person came to the altar, but it takes only one person to unleash revival. God used one person to bring revival to West Savannah.

I define revival as: "God pouring Himself on His people." For God to pour out Himself, He needs only one person who will unreservedly surrender everything to Him. At Westminster Presbyterian Church, that one person was a young mother who came forward in

---

I believed that when church people did four things, God would send revival: (1) humble themselves, (2) pray, (3) seek God's face and (4) repent.

---

response to my sermon. I had expected everyone in the church to come to the altar; she was the only one to respond to my sermon. That is why I said the sermon produced "poor" results.

To prepare for revival, my sermon that Sunday was based on the verse, "If my people, which are called by my name, shall humble themselves, and pray, and seek my face, and turn from their wicked ways; then will I hear from heaven, and will forgive their sin, and will heal their land" (2 Chron. 7:14, *KJV*).

I believed that when church people did four things, God would send revival: (1) humble themselves, (2) pray, (3) seek God's face and (4) repent.

I wanted more than an evangelistic crusade; I wanted revival. Technically, an evangelistic crusade takes place when the gospel is preached with a view of evangelizing the lost. A revival is God's spirit being poured out on His people (i.e., God touches the people, and they in turn touch Him).

Praying for Revival

In preparation for my sermon about revival, I sneaked away each morning to pray at a city park in the Gordston area, a park where no one ever seemed to go. I arrived at the city park each morning at 6:00 to intercede for my sermon about revival.

Whereas sometimes I feel heaven is shut up and my prayers

don't get through, during those early morning times of prayer prior to the evangelistic crusade, I felt as though my prayers were getting through to God. I felt God was hearing and would give us a great crusade. Because of this, I was disappointed when only one lady came to the altar that Sunday morning.

After praying for a week, I preached the sermon based on 2 Chronicles 7:14, concluding by calling everyone in the church to come to the altar to pray for revival. In my mind, I could see many people at the altar. I could see every person in the audience getting out of his or her pew, walking forward and kneeling at the altar, crying out for revival. Nothing happened, however. No one responded.

I made the invitation clear: "Come forward and pray for revival."

The invitation was aimed at everyone: Sunday School teachers, leaders, fathers and mothers.

"Everyone come to the altar and pray for revival."

The statement was clear, but no one came to the altar.

We sang the first verse of the invitation song, and no one came. The lack of response surprised me because in my prayer time I had convinced myself people would come, and the altar would be filled.

We sang a second verse and no one came. My confidence began to evaporate.

Where are the results for which I prayed? I questioned.

Then it happened: A young mother came forward and knelt at the altar. She began to weep.

No one came to pray with the young mother. After we finished singing, I went and stood beside her, shaking her hand.

"Thank you for coming," I commented. "God will answer your prayer."

Little did I know this young woman's prayer was intended for many of her relatives to get saved.

That Sunday afternoon this young mother left her children with their father and went to every house in West Savannah, telling everyone, "You just gotta come to the church and get saved."

I was later told that she cried in most of the homes. They were genuine tears of concern for the people in each house.

The Crusade's Lasting Effects

The revival meeting was a great success, and to this day I credit part of its effectiveness to the young mother who went door-to-door to canvass the neighborhood. Thirty-seven people prayed to receive Christ during the crusade. Although the numbers are not great compared to the thousands converted in a Billy Graham crusade, for a

---

Although the numbers are not great compared to the thousands converted in a Billy Graham crusade, for a church averaging approximately 100 in attendance, we thought 37 conversions were as great as the events on the Day of Pentecost.

---

church averaging approximately 100 in attendance, we thought 37 conversions were as great as the events on the Day of Pentecost.

To this day, Earl McQuay, the evangelist who preached at those meetings, looks back on the crusade, saying, "This was the greatest crusade I ever preached."

Earl does not mean the greatest in number of conversions and surely not the greatest in the size of the crowd, but the greatest in the demonstration of the power of God.

Earl had worked all summer and at first was reluctant to take off from his job to come to Savannah to preach a revival. I did not promise him a specific amount of money, and he needed money to return to school in the fall.

In those days, room, board and tuition at Columbia Bible College for an entire semester cost only $315. Whereas Earl had worked all summer to save for college, he barely made a dent in what he needed for the fall semester. In the providence of God, the love offering came to $315, enough to pay his entire fall semester bill.

A month earlier no one came to the church on the first day of Vacation Bible School (VBS) because I thought if I planned a good program, the children would come. I thought people praying was all that was needed to have a great week of VBS. My failure at VBS taught me the necessity of marketing and communication. A month after VBS, I advertised the evangelistic crusade, and in contrast to

Vacation Bible School, enough people came the first night to fill the church sanctuary.

If You Plan It Properly, They Will Come

As I approached the evangelistic crusade, I determined not to have an empty auditorium. So I began to advertise to attract people to the meetings. I had a flyer printed announcing Earl McQuay, a dynamic young evangelist from Columbia Bible College, as the speaker. Earl was my classmate, and I had seen the power of God upon him in the street meetings in Columbia, South Carolina. I organized the junior boys of the Sunday School. I gave them boxes of tacks and flyers and told them to tack an announcement on every light pole, tree and fence in the neighborhood.

They obeyed and literally wallpapered West Savannah with mimeographed flyers.

A printer from Independent Presbyterian Church heard about the evangelistic crusade and volunteered to print invitations. The invitations he printed for the evangelistic crusade looked like wedding invitations. A line was provided at the bottom of each invitation for church members to write their names; this way friends knew who had mailed the invitations.

"Write the name of the person you are inviting to the evangelistic crusade on the invitation." Then I instructed, "There is a place for you to sign your name."

A list of every person in the neighborhood was taped onto the rear church door. I asked everyone in the church to sign up to mail an invitation to a neighbor, then phone the neighbor, finally visit the neighbor and invite the neighbor to the evangelistic crusade.

"Every person in the neighborhood should come to the crusade at least once," I exhorted.

This was Earl McQuay's first evangelistic crusade, and it was the first time I had conducted a crusade. Earl McQuay later became vice president of Columbia Bible College, teaching courses in evangelism, Bible and practical theology.

A Chain of Prayer

The crusade began on a Monday night. Only one lady—a young mother—had come to the altar on Sunday morning. I announced on

Sunday that a prayer meeting would begin at 6:00 A.M. on Monday morning.

"Drop by the church on your way to work; pray with us for revival," I explained. "We don't all have to pray at the same time, but if we all prayed, God will send revival."

"As soon as you pray, leave for work," I exhorted.

That first Monday morning at 6:00 A.M. the sun had not yet risen. Earl and I arrived at the church at that gray time between the darkness of night and the brightness of sunrise.

Promptly at 6:00 in the morning, Earl and I stood at the church altar—no one else was there. Because I was an "on-time person," I wanted to start promptly at 6:00—whether or not anyone else came to pray with us.

I read the Scriptures and explained to Earl that the key to revival was the spirit of God being poured on His people. Then we knelt at the altar and I began praying. Still no one was there to pray with us.

When I finished, Earl began praying. While he was praying, I heard the creak of the church door and footsteps on the rug coming down the center aisle. I did not want to be disrespectful and look up from praying.

Someone knelt beside Earl, then that person prayed, and soon another, and another, and another and another came to pray.

Thereafter we held a prayer meeting at the church altar every morning of the crusade from 6:00 A.M. to 7:30 A.M.

Although a large crowd of people never came at once to pray, someone was always there to pray next. A chain of prayer stretched from 6:00 A.M. past 7:30 A.M., praying for the lost people of West Savannah.

We learned that prayer changes things, and was a key to the success of my first revival meeting at Westminster Presbyterian Church.

PRINCIPLES TO TAKE AWAY

1. *The principle of the power of one dedicated person.* Many ministers look for a large number of people to do the work of God, but a great work for God can be done by one person who is completely dedicated to God. It takes only one per-

son to release God's power in any given event. We are told, "Who has despised the day of small things?" (Zech. 4:10), and this one person did more to bring revival than all the other planning and advertising I did.

2. *The principle of the unexpected prayer return.* I preached a sermon expecting every person in the audience to come and kneel in prayer. Now I realize that ego was wrapped up in my desire to see an altar filled with people. God answered my prayer and gave spiritual power, but not through many people praying at the altar. Through one person, "the glory of the Lord appeared to all the congregation" (Num. 16:19).

3. *The principle of God's unexpected supply.* Whereas Earl McQuay had worked all summer to earn money to pay for his Bible college bill, in one week of dedicated service, he received a love offering large enough to pay his entire room, board and tuition for one semester at Columbia Bible College. God supplied for Earl McQuay as he in turn gave all his abilities to the Lord without reserve.

"My mother and two of the Mrs. Smiths"

14

Ice Cream Paid for My First Car

Savannah is known for its four o'clock "gully washers" on a summer afternoon. Somewhere around 4:00 P.M., the bottom of the sky usually drops out and it rains for 15 minutes. Yet 30 minutes later the sun will shine again and by dinnertime children are playing in the street, and men are playing softball after dinner.

Because I knew about the four o'clock gully washers, I was not concerned one Wednesday afternoon about being stuck at home. I knew the rain would pass, and by church time I could ride my English racing bike across town to West Savannah. Except, this particular Wednesday it kept raining and raining and raining.

"Lord, stop the rain so I can get to prayer meeting," I prayed frantically.

God did not answer my prayer, though, at least not the way I wanted answers.

One hour before prayer meeting I was still frantically pacing up and down the front porch, waiting for the rain to stop. I had to lead the prayer meeting at 7:00 P.M., and it took 35 minutes to ride seven miles across town.

I couldn't ride in the rain. An English racing bicycle is a peculiar contraption, especially on wet streets. It has no fenders so the front wheel spits dirty water off the pavement between your legs up to the front of your shirt. The back wheel heaves dirty water up your backbone and across your shoulders. If you ride slow enough, it will not splash water; but that is not possible when you have to ride seven miles across Savannah, Georgia, in a short time period.

I was too sophisticated to wear swimming trunks and dash through the rain to West Savannah; what would the people say about their "Preacher" zipping up to the church in swimming trunks? No way!

Getting to the Church on Time

I finally decided I should leave in spite of the rain so I could reach the church on time for the prayer meeting. So I covered my good ministerial trousers with plastic laundry bags, tying them tightly around my ankles. Then, pulling another laundry bag over my head, and wrapping still more laundry bags around my arms, I tucked my Bible in my belt and took off across Savannah for prayer meeting.

The laundry bags worked *almost* perfectly; but they did not work perfectly. The dirty street water splashed where the bags met at my waist and trickled down inside my legs, making me look as though I had an accident. From the back wheel dirty water splashed up underneath the bag to the back of my white starched shirt.

When I arrived at the church, I locked my bike in back of the church and made a mad dash through the side door to the men's room. I tried to sponge off dirt with paper towels, but Savannah dirt does not come off white starched shirts.

The prayer meeting had already started; what was I going to do? I rationalized, *If I can get behind the pulpit without anyone seeing me, they won't know how dirty the front of my trousers look.*

Faster than a brisk walk, I turned my back to the audience and walked sideways to the pulpit and began the song service. It was

---

It was obvious to everyone—I was a mess.

Mrs. Miller kept gawking over her hymnbook,

trying to look around the edge of the pulpit.

---

obvious to everyone—I was a mess. Mrs. Miller kept gawking over her hymnbook, trying to look around the edge of the pulpit.

"Your Preacher Is a Sloppy Mess"

Through the years I learned that when you have made a mess, rather than trying to hide your mess, admit it. Sometimes being honest will disarm people; sometimes they will even like you more because of your transparency.

So I stepped from behind the pulpit for the congregation to see me, and said, "Your preacher is a sloppy mess."

I expected the people to laugh, but they sympathetically identified with me, more in embarrassment than in humor.

What was a "loss of face" was actually an opportunity for the Lord to arrange for the people in the church to purchase my first car. I had no clue, however, what was happening. I made it through prayer meeting, and afterward laughed together with some people about my looks.

Nixing a Ladies' Bake Sale

The following Sunday morning after church, Mrs. Smith, the president of the Ladies' Auxiliary, came to talk to me: "We're going to have a bake sale..."

"No, no, no..." I quickly interrupted her.

I explained to her that only liberal churches had bake sales to raise money for missions, and that Westminster Presbyterian Church would give sacrificially. I went on to explain that we should support missions, but only with the voluntary gifts of God's people. From a heart of deep sincerity I explained why bake sales compromised Christianity.

"I don't know of any fundamental church that would have a bake sale," I announced with finality.

"We didn't mean to harm anything," Mrs. Smith quickly added.

"The Ladies' Auxiliary won't have a bake sale," she then assured me.

I was surprised how quickly the battle was won. Certain things made me bold, and this was one of them. I spoke authoritatively, and without forked tongue. Mrs. Smith understood what I said, and I was sure she would tell the other ladies in the church about my decision.

"Have Some Ice Cream, Preacher"

The following Saturday I rode the train to Savannah, and boarded a bus to Westminster Presbyterian Church in West Savannah. One of the younger Miller girls was on the bus with me, just a primary tot.

I was passing pleasantries with the girl when all of a sudden she giggled, dropped her head and blurted out, "Preacher, we've got a surprise for you."

I did not pay much attention to her disclosure. The church people were always inviting me to their houses for a meal, and I just assumed this was another invitation.

I got off the bus approximately one block from the church, at the corner of Fourth and Augusta Road. From a block away I could see a crowd of people around the church. I wondered what was going on. A little barefooted boy in short pants came running down the street to me, grabbed my hand, and pulled me toward the church.

"Guess what?" he laughed his question to me.

"What?"

"I can't tell you."

He dropped my hand and ran back to the church.

By now I was curious about the surprise, hearing about it from both the little girl on the bus and the little boy who just spoke to me.

On one occasion I arrived at the church to find out I had to conduct a funeral, and on another occasion I found several families cutting the grass. I wondered what was happening now. When I got closer, it was evident.

They're churning ice cream on the church porch, I said to myself.

Before I could say anything, Mrs. Smith yelled out, "We're not selling cakes." Her voice giggled with anticipation.

"The Ladies Auxiliary is not sponsoring this...this...ice cream churn," Mrs. Miller's raspy voice outechoed Mrs. Smith's voice.

I was dumbfounded. Ten or 12 ladies from the church were busily selling ice cream. The edge of the porch was covered with white table cloths. Ice cream bowls from various sets of dishes—represent-

---

"We're going to buy you a car," Mrs. Smith announced victoriously. I was stunned; I was speechless. The preacher who was known for speaking did not have a word to say.

---

ing many homes in the neighborhood—were set up on the porch, and none of the spoons matched. The ice cream in some of the churns was hard and it was packed down waiting for customers.

"What's going on?" I threw the question out to anyone in general.

"We're going to buy you a car," Mrs. Smith announced victoriously.

All the ladies laughed as friends do who are surprising another friend with a gift. The children cheered.

"Have some ice cream, Preacher," Mrs. Smith said, pushing a bowl of vanilla ice cream into my hands.

I was stunned; I was speechless. The preacher who was known for speaking did not have a word to say.

I was against bake sales to raise money for the church, and they had agreed to my pronouncement. Cakes were nowhere in sight. They were selling ice cream to dozens of children. They were not doing this for the church; they were doing this for me.

As I surveyed the churchyard, I observed, "There are more children here than there are in Sunday School; we ought to serve ice cream in Sunday School."

I spoke from the top of my head and from the bottom of my heart without thinking. If I had thought through what I had said in jest, I would have realized what the ladies of the church would do.

Ice cream was served in Sunday School the following day.

Back to the front porch of the church. The ladies had been selling ice cream for three hours, and they had two more hours to go, according to their schedule.

I sat on the front steps of the church for more than an hour, talking to people I had never seen before and who had never visited the church. I probably had more pastoral contact at the ice cream sale than if I had visited door-to-door.

My First Car: A Gift from God

After two Saturdays of ice cream sales, the ladies presented a $175 check to me for my first car. Mrs. Silla Hair had received permission to give me the check in the morning service, and everyone stood and applauded. Mr. Seckinger and Mr. Strickland, the church elders, had agreed to the presentation.

"This is from the people of West Savannah," Mrs. Hair was careful to point out, "not from the church!"

My first car was a 1939 two-door Chevy coupe, and had a rumble seat area. The rumble seat, however, had been removed. During World War II a small-dairy farmer was unable to buy a truck so he converted this '39 Chevy coupe into a truck by lining the back seat and rumble seat area with mahogany. The car looked like a coupe, but when the trunk door was open, it was roomy enough to hold the milk cans and haul them to the dairy.

I bought the car at the local Chevrolet company for $175, and paid only $2 for title registration. In those days taxes did not have to be paid on cars.

When I was driving up and down the streets of Savannah, people remarked, "There goes our pastor."

They seemed to be proud of me.

Then they added a second phrase, "There goes our car."

Although the money for the car was given to me as a gift, the people of West Savannah considered it their car. I considered it a gift from God; and used it for the people of West Savannah.

PRINCIPLES TO TAKE AWAY

1. *The principle of supplying our needs before we ask.* I was perfectly willing to pastor Westminster Presbyterian Church by riding my bicycle, riding a bus and driving Mr. Miller's car. A time came, however, when I needed my own automobile, and God provided it through the ladies of the church. I should have realized my need, and prayed for a car. Yet for some reason my self-esteem was not strong enough to think I was worthy of a car, and my faith was weak so I could not ask for a car.

2. *The principle that man's extremity is God's opportunity.* The ladies of Westminster Presbyterian Church probably would not have purchased the car if I had not stood in front of them a soaking mess at prayer meeting. Although I was laughing, they were probably ashamed of what had happened, motivating them to provide the money gift for my first car.

"My first loves: Gertrude and Ruth"

15

A Boy's First Love: Gertrude

I told a joke about Gertrude; it was actually a story with a punch line. The people of West Savannah loved my story about Gertrude. Because they liked it so much, they asked me to repeat the story at church suppers, youth meetings and at dinner tables when I visited in their homes for a meal.

The people liked my story about Gertrude so much that they named my first car Gertrude. The best way for you to understand how much the people of West Savannah became attached to the name "Gertrude" is to tell the story to you.

The Saga of Gertrude

I was walking down the railroad track with Gertrude...she were mine own true love. We held hands, swinging our arms back and forth like small children. It was a beautiful day to be walking with someone you loved, and the one who loved you. Everything was perfect for our love to bloom and grow.

The sun was up...the grass was riz...and the bird was on the wing....My word...how absurd...I thought the wing was on the bird.

"Gertrude...I love you with all my heart," I told her.

I waited for those warm words from her. I wanted her to tell me she loved me.

I waited...and I waited...and I waited...but Gertrude didn't say a word.

"Don't you love me?" I asked. "When I said I loved you, you should tell me that you love me."

I waited...and I waited...and I waited...but Gertrude didn't say a word.

"See that beautiful tree over in the meadow?" I pointed awkwardly to the tree. "Do you think it's beautiful?" I asked.

I waited...and waited...and waited...but Gertrude didn't say a word.

"See that beautiful creek over on the other side of the railroad track?" I pointed with my other hand awkwardly. "Do you think the creek is beautiful?" I asked.

I waited...and waited...and waited...but Gertrude didn't say a word.

"Gertrude, I think I hear a train coming," I warned. The train could smash us to smithereens. "Don't you think we ought to get off the track?" I asked.

I waited...and waited...and waited...but Gertrude didn't say a word.

"Wo-o-o-o, wo-o-o-o!!!" a train whistled in the distance.

"Gertrude, the train is getting closer." I was getting more and more worried. I warned her again. "It's on this very track. We'd better get off this track," I again warned.

I waited...and waited...and waited...Gertrude didn't say a word.

I looked back and the train was bearing down on us, fast. "It's coming fast. We'd better jump for our lives," I continued to warn her. I was scared we'd both be killed.

I waited...and waited...and waited... but Gertrude didn't say a word.

"Wo-o-o-o, wo-o-o-o!!!" the whistle got louder.

"Jump, Gertrude!" I yelled as the train barreled down on us. I jumped clear of the oncoming danger. But Gertrude kept on walking.

I waited...and waited...and waited...but Gertrude didn't say a word.

The train smashed her. She disintegrated in every direction. Her body parts flew in every direction as I jumped to safety. As the train roared past, I wondered what happened to her.

Pointing awkwardly to the tree, I said, "There's her leg."

Pointing awkwardly to the meadow, I said, "There's her arm."

Pointing awkwardly to the creek, I said, "There's her torso."

Looking to my feet I saw her two ears. I picked up the two ears with one ear in each hand and shook them as one would shake the crumbs off a napkin.

Then holding the ears up before me, I said, "Gertrude...Gertrude...can you hear me?"

And I waited...and waited...and waited...but Gertrude didn't say a word.

West Savannah Loved Gertrude

I never thought the story was as funny as the people of West Savannah did. Maybe it is because I knew the punch line, such as it was. As I visited in the homes of the unchurched, they constantly asked me to tell the story of Gertrude. So I repeated the story in many homes.

When the whole community bought ice cream on the front porch of Westminster Presbyterian Church, they knew the money was being used for the preacher's new car. The ladies of West Savannah raised $175 and gave it to me during a Sunday morning service.

Within a couple of days, I purchased a 1939 Chevy coupe with a rumble seat. As explained in the last chapter, the rumble seat had been removed by the previous owner, so I could only transport two people in the front seat—one in the driver's seat and one in the passenger's seat.

Every time I was heading to town, I stopped by the bus stop to pick up anyone from West Savannah needing a ride downtown. The older people sat in the front seat, and everyone else had to sit on the floor in the rear compartment. So I kept four or five little stools in the back compartment for passengers to use. The rumble seat was wide open, hair was waving in the breeze, so everyone seemed to enjoy the short two-mile ride to downtown.

During one of these trips I was taking the youngest of the five Mrs. Smiths from Westminster Presbyterian Church to town. Mrs. Smith and her three children were sitting in the backseat.

I told Mrs. Smith, "This car is like a girlfriend; it's like a boy's first love."

"Then I am going to call her 'Gertrude,' because she won't say a word," Mrs. Smith said laughingly.

The name "Gertrude" stuck.

From that moment on the 1939 Chevy was called "Gertrude" by everyone in West Savannah; and because a boy's first car is like his first love, I loved Gertrude.

"Here comes the preacher and Gertrude," people commented as I rumbled down the street with the rumble seat wide open.

PRINCIPLES TO TAKE AWAY

1. *The principle of leadership identification.* When followers like their leader, they identify with him and his success. The people of West Savannah liked me, and rejoiced in my new car. They liked it so much that they called it "Gertrude."

2. *The principle of sharing your blessing.* I was appreciative of the car the people of West Savannah gave me. Every time I drove into town, I went past the bus stop, picked up people and drove them to town. This did more than show appreciation; it helped me to serve my community. In the spirit of the "cup of cold water" (Matt. 10:42) Jesus told us to give in His name. I gave Gertrude to the people for their use, and they responded by being saved.

"Dreams came true, and dreams died"

16

The Illusion of Dreams That Keep Us Going

I looked through the rain-sprinkled windows of the auditorium of Westminster Presbyterian Church at four weed-filled lots next to the church. I wanted that piece of ground for the church. Of all the things I prayed for—and did not get—I desperately wanted the four lots so we could expand the church.

I closed my eyes and saw a beautiful Sunday School building; it was gleaming white, had green shingles and a paved parking lot. It was the most beautiful Sunday School building I had ever seen. I could see it sitting on those four lots. That building in my mind was as real as the rain pouring down the windows.

You can't achieve what you can't conceive, so I dreamed of a beautiful Sunday School building—not an empty building. The porches and rooms were filled with laughing children.

The sky was steel gray; rain had been falling intermittently all day. My dreary spirit reflected the dreary day. The sandy streets of West Savannah had turned to mud and it was cold and damp; I felt like a captive in the church building. I did not want to run through the rain, going from house to house to visit people in the neighborhood. So I stood in the sanctuary looking through the rain-spattered windows at the four lots next door.

"Lord, give me those four lots so I can build a large sanctuary," I prayed.

I had prayed this prayer to God on many occasions. I did not have a lot of faith that I would get the lots, so I did not pray with assurance, but I had a deep desire. I was like a little kid begging for something he knows he won't get.

The four lots were located right behind Westminster Presbyterian Church on Third Street, each measuring 100 feet long. They cost more money than I could trust God for—they cost $100 each. My faith was small and $400 for four lots was bigger than I could see or really believe. If anything, the four lots and Sunday School convicted me of my "little faith."

If Jesus had been physically standing there, He would have said, "O ye of little faith" (Matt. 6:30, *KJV*).

The Westminster sanctuary at one time seated more than 500 people, but when the attendance declined, the sanctuary was divided into classrooms, offices, rest rooms and a hallway. Now the down-sized sanctuary seated about 150. My dream was to remove all the walls and fill the 500 seats with warm bodies. I could see 500 people filling the sanctuary, listening to me preach the Word of God. I could see people packed into the 500 seats and standing around by the walls.

I closed my eyes and saw me standing where the pulpit used to be. The pulpit in the future would be high, much higher than it was now. The balcony had been closed off, so when I remodeled the sanctuary I would open the balcony for 100 people to sit there and listen to me preach.

On that cold rainy afternoon, I could see the sanctuary of Westminster Presbyterian Church return to its former glory days. One large sanctuary, and the stained-glass windows restored to their glory. It would also include a large organ that could rattle windows when its deep tones were being played.

To me, a church of 500 people was the largest church in the world. My vision as a 20-year-old preacher was 500 people. I just could not see myself preaching in any building larger than what would contain that many people, or ministering to more people than that.

A Lack of Faith

On a sunny afternoon of another day, I was eating dinner in the Green family's home. What Mrs. Green said about these four lots made me choke on the fried chicken.

"We ought to buy those four lots in back of the church so we can

---

My lack of faith kept me quiet. I was intimidated. I did not want my dream to be a "me, too" added to what [Mrs. Green] had just said.

---

have room to expand for all the people who are coming to the church," she suggested at the table.

I should have shouted "Amen!" I should have told her that was my dream. I should have told her I was praying daily for those four lots. My lack of faith kept me quiet. I was intimidated. I did not want my dream to be a "me, too" added to what she had just said.

I also thought they might think it was ego or bragging if I told them about a filled church of 500 people.

As a young preacher I constantly struggled with self. It seemed every day I knocked Christ off the throne of my heart. If I talked about a church of 500, or talked about buying four lots to build Sunday School rooms, people might think I was bragging.

So I just quietly prayed about my dream.

A Missed Chance to Share the Vision

The day before Easter in 1953, I arrived at the church on Saturday morning to see a farmer on his tractor cutting the grass of the four lots in the back of the church building. Mr. Miller was standing by the back door of the church, yelling at the top of his voice over the roar of the tractor.

"Cut it as short as possible!" he repeated his command with a yell. "Cut it short so people can park in the field."

I had not thought about using the field for parking; the four lots were knee deep in weeds. The kids had cut a path through the middle of the field, but when the farmer cut the grass close to the ground, I saw the field was flat and level ground perfect for parking.

Westminster Presbyterian Church did not have one parking space. The church was located on a 100-foot lot, and the sanctuary was built to within 10 feet of the property line. So visitors who drove to the church parked on both sides of Fourth Avenue, or on Alexander Street. The street had no curbs, only dirt streets, so every once in a while somebody parked on the church grass. Because of the constant haranguing of the elders Seckinger and Strickland, I tried to keep everyone from parking on the grass in the front of the church.

Mr. Miller paid the farmer $5 for cutting the four lots.

Then he said to me, "We've got people driving from Nathaniel Greene housing projects for Easter services." He beamed about the excitement of a filled church.

Then Miller added, "They'll be driving from a mile away; they'll need a place to park tomorrow."

Miller then explained that families were coming from the other side of Highway 17 and he wanted them to park in the field.

We could see a small dust cloud of dry cut grass hovering over the four lots.

Mr. Miller looked at the field and said, "The church ought to buy these four lots."

He scratched his head trying to read my thoughts. "They're not going to cost too much, probably $100 a lot."

I should have shared with Mr. Miller my vision of purchasing the lots, but I did not do it. I should have described to him my vision of a Sunday School building with green shingles and gutters, but I did not do it. I should have described 500 people filling the old sanctuary, but I did not do it.

A Lack of Leadership Ability

The four lots were a dream that was constantly in my thoughts, but as a young preacher I did not understand the power of dreams. I did not understand that when followers buy into your dreams, they buy into your leadership. I did not understand the power of vision. If I had understood the first law of leadership, I might have motivated the congregation to purchase the four lots. The first law of leader-

---

The first law of leadership simply states: When people buy into your dreams, they buy into your leadership.

---

ship simply states: When people buy into your dreams, they buy into your leadership.

"Lord, why don't you give us those four lots?" I poured out my dreams to God.

At times in my early morning prayer, I agonized before God, wondering why he did not answer my prayers. Although he answered many prayers for conversion of lost people, this was one request He seemed to ignore.

One day while studying, I read that God told Abraham to walk through the ground to possess it. Being moved by my sermon, I left the church and walked to the four lots behind Westminster Presbyterian Church. I did not want people to know what I was doing, so I walked down Alexander Street, turned left down Third Avenue and walked the 400 feet in front of the empty lots.

The weeds were growing high between the last lot and the Arnstorff's house, preventing me from walking the final boundary of the four lots. So I turned and walked catty-corner back through the lots down the path made by the kids. As I walked, I prayed and asked God to give me the property.

Going back into my office, I continued to pray for the lots, asking God to give them to me. My prayers, however, mocked me. I had just been challenged by the faith of Abraham to walk around the property, but I let a few weeds next to the Arnstorff's house stop me.

I did not walk completely around the property; I left off one side of the property. Later, I was sure my lack of obedience in walking ALL THE WAY AROUND THE PROPERTY would keep me from getting the ground.

After I left the pastorate at Westminster Presbyterian Church, I thought about the four lots on many occasions. I thought about standing at the sanctuary window and looking at the four lots. They will always be an unfulfilled dream of mine.

As I look back at the four lots, I always blame my lack of faith or my lack of intercession. In time, however, I realized it was not a lack of faith or a lack or prayer; it was my lack of leadership ability.

If I had honestly wanted the property, I should have *first* communicated the dream to the people. *Second*, I should have given them an opportunity to buy into my dream and pray with me. *Third*, I should have given them an opportunity to contribute money toward the dream. *Finally*, I should have asked the church board to purchase the property. Because I did not understand leadership, I did none of these things and the dream died.

PRINCIPLES TO TAKE AWAY

1. *The principle of the impossible.* We will never discover what God can do until we attempt the impossible. I had vision and desire, but was afraid to act on them. As a result, God was never able to complete the vision.
2. *The principle of courage.* My problem was fear, which is the opposite of courage. I had never experienced buying property, so I thought it was a much greater task than it was. Later in life I purchased many pieces of property, and today I look back at my lack of faith and laugh. I should have had courage to attempt a task I thought was impossible so God could have answered my prayer and demonstrated His ability to answer prayer.
3. *The principle of biblical faith.* I thought I had faith because I believed in God, but my faith was extremely weak. If I had possessed faith in God, I would have acted on it. The old farmer said, "What's in the well, comes up in the bucket." If I had possessed biblical faith, I would have acted in an

obedient way, but the fear in my heart kept me from pursuing my dream.

4. *The principle of unfulfilled dreams.* No one will achieve all his or her dreams, but without dreams, a person won't do as much. No one can achieve every dream he or she has had, but dreams keep us going and dreams make the journey worthwhile. Although I never realized the dream of purchasing the four lots, that dream, and other dreams, motivated me to continued ministry. Although I did not realize that dream, other accomplishments were influenced by it.

5. *The principle of dream consensus.* When you have a dream that comes from God, others are probably also seeing the same thing. The leader's role is to dream. So leaders should look for confirmation for their dreams in others, then share their dreams so others can become a part of them.

> See the dream
> Buy the dream
> Own the dream
> Share the dream

"The 'Preacher' rocks the flock"

17

The Coat Thrower

I have had several nicknames in my life—the one I like most of all is "Preacher." I am not sure, though, how effective I was as a minister at Westminster Presbyterian Church. I not only looked young, I was young—too young for effective empathy with the sick, dying and those in deep need. I could not be called "Reverend" because I was not yet ordained, and no one called me "Pastor." Other names were given to pastors, such as "bishop," "elder" and some curse words used in anger. The term that was most endearing to me, however, was characterized by what I did best: I was the "Preacher."

For a short time period my congregation also called me "the Coat Thrower."

Now that is an interesting title; why would people call their pastor "the Coat Thrower"? Did he throw a coat on the floor while making a pastoral visit? Did he play a game at the Sunday School picnic and win the "coat-throwing contest"?

No, I was called "the Coat Thrower" for another reason.

To understand why, you have to examine the mind of a 19-year-old preacher, and ask a deeper question: "Where did he get his sermons?"

By all standards of community response, the people at Westminster Presbyterian Church liked my preaching, and the church grew because people liked my preaching and they came Sunday morning and Sunday night to hear my preaching. They liked it so much that everyone—members and nonmembers—called me "Preacher."

My Sermon Sources

So where did I get these sermons my congregation liked so much?

While a student at Columbia Bible College, I was constantly listening for any story that could spice up my sermons. I knew that people liked stories, remembered stories, were motivated by them and laughed at my funny stories. So I had my ears tuned for stories, events I could include in my preaching. I took careful notes in all my classes, carefully writing any story in the left-hand margins of my note paper. I considered great stories the meat of my sermons.

My best sermons came from the Bible classes that immersed me in Bible study. Obviously, when I studied the book of John, I preached from John. The same pattern followed with Daniel, Revelation, Romans and Genesis.

While attending classes during the week, I filled up my bucket, and on Sundays I poured out the Word of God into the hearts of my listeners in West Savannah.

At Columbia Bible College I attended five chapels a week, in addition to another 8 to 12 semester hours of Bible and doctrine classes.

So I sprinkled several stories throughout my messages, outlining my sermons on 3x5-inch cards. I still have many of these sermons filed away in a manila envelope, including the 3x5-inch cards, my original handwritten notes and a few typed outlines I took to the pulpit with me.

Exhilarated by British Flair

So where did the title "the Coat Thrower" originate?

After I had been at Westminster Presbyterian Church for about six months, I heard a British speaker at Columbia Bible College. He was a revivalist, an enthusiast and very emotional. Several British speakers came to the college each year, and most were known for their sedate sermons, whereby they reasoned from the Word of God. Most Britishers controlled themselves in the pulpit. Never would you say a Britisher was emotional or revivalistic.

This particular British homiletician was a big-boned man, his large head was covered with golden curly hair, he had a hawk nose and his eyes pierced the listeners.

What that preacher did to me in chapel I instantly wanted to do to the people of West Savannah. What I considered to be a great sermon would be just as great when I preached the following Sunday.

I admired his blue-striped shirt and solid-blue tie. So I bought a blue-striped shirt and solid-blue tie just like his. I liked what I felt when I heard him preach, so I wanted to look just like him. I wanted my audience to feel the same way about me when I preached.

The British pulpiteer described Joseph wearing the coat of many colors. I could see Joseph walking over the hills toward his 10 brothers. Using vivid narrative and whispered tones, the British accent repeated the words of the brothers.

"Take that blasphemous coat of many colors from him and smear it in mud."

"No," a second brother cited. "Let's dip it in blood," he reasoned. "Mud can be washed out, but never blood."

"Let's dip it in his own blood," another brother spit out the words, seeing the hatred in the eyes of his brother that reflected his own animosity.

"Let's do it," they all agreed.

The speaker lifted me up out of my chapel seat. I floated back to the Palestinian hills to survey the mob scene of 10 brothers viciously attacking young Joseph. They grabbed him, they spit on him, they slapped him, they kicked him and they stripped him of a beautiful coat of many colors.

In an instantaneous liquid movement, the speaker shed his coat from his broad shoulders, rolled it viciously into a ball and heaved it into the rear corner of the platform.

I was lifted to a pinnacle, then I crashed into the corner of the chapel platform, wrapped in that coat. I had so identified with the act of preaching that when the coat was heaved into the corner, I felt hatred for the assault on Joseph by the 10 brothers.

What that preacher did to me in chapel I instantly wanted to do to the people of West Savannah. What I considered to be a great sermon would be just as great when I preached the following Sunday.

Envisioning Sensational Dramatics

As I was preparing my sermon, I painted a mental picture seeing myself lifting the people of West Savannah to hate the 10 brothers' actions toward Joseph. I wanted them to feel what I felt, to hear it the way I heard it, to experience it the way I experienced it.

Now more than 40 years later, I do not remember the point or thesis of the Britisher's sermon. I do not know whether it was a sermon to call young people to dedicate their lives to Jesus Christ, or a call to prayer, or a call to separation or a call to patience. I do not remember why he threw the coat other than to evoke a crowd response.

Neither do I remember the purpose of my sermon. Most of my sermons did not have a well-conceived purpose. I just put together a great Bible lesson, explained the Bible, illustrated it with stories and closed in prayer.

When I closed in prayer, I always invited people to walk forward and kneel at the altar. I always asked people to receive Christ as Savior. In the next part of my invitation, I asked young people to surrender their lives to Jesus Christ—to put everything on the altar. If I focused on any other particular points of the sermon, I usually asked the people to commit themselves to prayer, to read their Bibles, to share Christ with someone or to improve their Christian homes.

I would like you to think I threw the coat from the pulpit of Westminster Presbyterian Church because it contributed to the point of the sermon I preached about Joseph and his 10 brothers. I can't say that, though. I threw the coat for the sensational results I wanted my hearers to feel when I came to that dramatic moment.

I wanted to be successful, sensational and effective; but when I became successful, sensational and effective, I did not know how to cope with it.

As I look back on that sermon, I now see pride written all over the act. I wanted people to feel toward me as I felt toward the Britisher. I had put him on a pedestal, and I wanted the people of West Savannah to also put me on a pedestal. I wanted them to think of me as a man of God. Although nothing is wrong with being a godly example to influence others, my motive was pride; I wanted people to think well of me. Remember, Jesus condemned the scribes and Pharisees because they wanted all men to think well of them.

Another problem I had as a young preacher was not knowing how to conduct myself in what I wanted. I wanted to be successful, sensational and effective; but when I became successful, sensational and effective, I did not know how to cope with it.

A Dramatic Coat-Throwing Presentation

The Sunday after I heard the impressive presentation at Columbia Bible College, I preached the sermon of Joseph and the 10 brothers at Westminster Presbyterian Church. I did not exactly copy the words of the British preacher, for that would be blatant plagiarism; but my sermon was veiled in plagiarism. I told the story my own way and added my own Southern twist; my Southern accent was obvious, and I revealed the immaturity of a college sophomore.

I emphasized Joseph's coat more than did the British preacher. I walked from behind the pulpit to stroke my coat as though it were long, pretending to be Joseph, and how he might have stroked his coat of many colors. I made more references to the coat of many colors than did my British idol. I wanted to make sure no one missed the point. I was trying to be as dramatic as my British counterpart, but was not as descriptive and eloquent; I was probably a lot more rural and crude.

Arriving at the dramatic apex of the sermon, I then repeated what I had heard the Britisher say: "They grabbed him, they spit on him, they slapped him, they beat him and they stripped him of the beautiful coat of many colors. Then, in an act of defiance they threw him into the pit."

Dramatically, I stripped off my coat much slower than had the Britisher. I did not want the people to miss what I was doing. Slowly I rolled my coat into a ball, then turning, I cast it against the back wall behind the pulpit.

My coat dropped to the platform floor.

My audience gasped, but not the way some might at a movie theater. They gasped as a person might suck air into the mouth, shaking their heads in unbelief.

Five or six people stood, pulling themselves up with their hands on the pew in front of them. Cocking their heads, they strained to see the coat on the floor. They responded more physically than I had anticipated. At Columbia Bible College the students responded inwardly, in their thoughts and hearts. In West Savannah, however, necks craned to see the coat. Heads bobbed to view the actual crumpled jacket on the floor.

"What did he do, Momma?" a little girl asked.

"Sh-h-h-h-h," Momma said.

When the sermon ended I was not wearing my coat, so I called one of the men to lead in prayer for the benediction. Then, when no one was looking, I retrieved my coat and put it back on.

The Adulation Was Overpowering

As people left the sanctuary and greeted me at the back door, they responded in a variety of ways.

"That was some preaching," one of the men shook my hand as he exited. "Some preaching."

He said exactly what I wanted to hear. I gulped deeply at his compliment, as a young boy would who is throwing down a Coca-Cola without coming up for air.

The compliment—oh, it was good!

"You really got into that sermon, Preacher," one man laughed. Then correcting himself he added, "You really got out of that coat."

Some of us stood outside the church and talked about the visual lesson: how graphic, how memorable, how captivating.

That week I went to the corner grocery store one day.

The proprietor asked, "Did you really throw that coat against the wall?"

"Yup."

Because I liked the adulation so much, my mind went to work that week: What other story in the Bible refers to a coat?

My Obsession with "Coat" Sermons

The following week at Columbia Bible College I listed every biblical event I could think of that included a coat:

Jesus' robe.

Peter putting on his coat after fishing all night.

Jacob wrapping himself in a coat to sleep.

Paul asking for his coat.

The following week I preached a second sermon that included a dramatic coat-throwing episode. I would like to tell you the exact sermon topic I preached about that day, and describe how dramatically I ripped off my coat and presented an object lesson of a coat. I do not remember what I preached, however, but I did take off my coat.

Another time I preached about Peter fishing all night and catching no fish. When Peter saw Jesus coming, he reached under the seat of the boat to grab his coat. As I explained this, I put on my coat as though I were Peter. It really did not add much to the sermon, but it created a visual effect.

During the next three or four weeks, I preached several sermons that included taking off, putting on or throwing a coat. It seemed to be a good show, but I only continued it for about five sermons. Why? Because each time I dramatically went for the coat, I saw a decreasing effect of the dramatic. I heard no more gasps from the audience. No one stood to see what I was doing, and the heads were not bobbing to see the coat on the floor.

The people in the audience were nice, and the nicest thing they did was to say nothing. They did not make fun of me, nor did they tell me it was a great idea. After about three coat-throwing episodes, people stopped talking about it in the yard after church. I probably quit using the coat as a prop because people were no longer affected by its use.

A Neighborhood Reputation as the Coat Thrower

About the time I stopped using my coat for dramatics in my sermons, however, the people in the community who did not attend church started talking about it. The church members who had seen me throw my coat stopped talking about it; the people who did not come to church began to talk about the incident.

I realized coat throwing was an act, not a true reflection of the sermon. I remember trying to tell this neighborhood man, "Come see the Lord Jesus Christ, not to see a preacher throw his coat."

As I visited house to house, people asked, "Are you the one who threw the coat?"

Then they usually added a second question, "Did you really throw it on the floor?"

Obviously, it was sensational to throw a coat on the floor, and not every preacher has thrown his coat. Because I had done something unusual, people talked about it.

"I'll come hear you when you throw your coat again," one of the neighborhood men said.

I then realized coat throwing was an act, not a true reflection of the sermon. I remember trying to tell this neighborhood man he should attend church because of the message of the Word of God, not because of any of the preacher's theatrics.

"Come see the Lord Jesus Christ, not to see a preacher throw his coat."

I do not remember if the neighbor ever came to church.

Giving People Something to Believe

Today, my preaching would probably be characterized as substantive rather than formula. The overused event was the beginning of a change in the way I preached. I was finding it more and more difficult to find stories, so I naturally looked for substance to put into my sermons.

At about that time I also realized the Word of God changes lives. The people of God have to hear the Word of God. I found myself reading more commentaries to derive more meat from the Scriptures. I found myself replacing stories with Bible expositional content. I found myself preaching the Word of God rather than putting on an entertaining spectacle. Although my sermons became more Bible centered, and less sensational, I saw the messages having a greater influence in my listeners.

One of the reasons I later chose to attend Dallas Theological Seminary was that it trained men to preach the way I wanted to preach.

The founder of Dallas Theological Seminary once said, "You haven't preached the gospel until you have given people something to believe."

I wanted to give the people something to help change their lives.

PRINCIPLES TO TAKE AWAY

1. *The principle of deceptive methods.* Many have such a deep desire to serve the Lord that they turn to questionable methods to be effective in Christ's service. We should recognize, however, that "the heart is deceitful above all things, and desperately wicked" (Jer. 17:9). We should not heed our heart's desire for recognition, but allow our methods to come from the Word of God. We should attempt to put Christ first and our prayer should be—what

those seeking Jesus in the Bible said—"We would see Jesus" (John 12:21, *KJV*).

2. *The principle of unwanted success.* I wanted people to think of me as a sensational preacher who could influence their emotions. When I got what I wanted, I was unsettled by my success and uneasy because of its disruptive results.

3. *The principle of managed enthusiasm.* What my sermons lacked in substance and focus, they made up in enthusiasm and excitement. I wanted my hearers to feel the Word of God, and they did. Therefore, I purposely planned excitement, stories and involvement in every sermon to communicate to them "life, and that they may have it more abundantly" (John 10:10). Achieving success in this endeavor is evidenced by the name they gave me: "Preacher."

4. *The principle of excessive success.* I wanted my listeners to "feel" my sermons, and they did. I wanted to move them to action; they stood and gawked and they strained to see a coat on the floor. I was not satisfied, however, when I got what I sought. The excessiveness of my success led to changes in my preaching. Today, I place more emphasis on substance than on form. I attempt to preach the Word of God and let God change hearts by the power of His Word.

"I 'lived'—but also 'bombed'—in the pulpit"

18

When the Jar Breaks

Not only did I preach at the 11:00 A.M. worship service every Sunday morning, but I was also the Sunday School superintendent of the 10:00 A.M. Sunday School. As Sunday School superintendent, I thought my most important contribution was the "superintendent's devotional," which was a five-minute talk to the children.

From the smallest child to the oldest adult, everyone gathered in the main sanctuary for opening exercises. There we sang a couple of songs, celebrated birthdays and listened to the superintendent (me) present a devotional before dispersing to individual classes.

Many of the children in Sunday School did not stay for the worship service, so I thought the "superintendent's devotional" was my best opportunity to present the gospel to the young people and influence their lives.

Compliments Inspired Me

"I liked it when you used the disposable handkerchief," someone told me.

It was not a disposable handkerchief; it just turned into several colors as I pulled it through my hand. I had used a magical handkerchief in a devotional as a visual aid to hold their attention and to help the children see what I was explaining. The handkerchief turned from black to red to white to green. Similar to the description

---

"I like those flannelgraph lessons," an elderly man told me.... When he saw the pictures of the people in the Bible, he remembered the story better than when he heard a sermon.

---

of the Wordless Book, I did a magic trick with the handkerchief, explaining that the black part represented our sins, the red part described the blood of Christ, the white talked about cleansing our hearts from sin and the green symbolized eternal life.

"I like those flannelgraph lessons," an elderly man told me.

The man went on to explain that when he saw the pictures of the people in the Bible, he remembered the story better than when he heard a sermon. As a result, I tried to find an object lesson each week for my superintendent's message.

Planning the "Really Big Show"

After one year of planning object lessons every week, the well was beginning to run dry. So for one particular Sunday morning I thought of an object lesson that would show Christ taking our penalty for sin.

The object lesson was simple and involved three things: first, a red hammer, which represented judgment; second, a jar, representing Christ; third, a small figurine representing sinners.

I painted a hammer bright red and used adhesive tape to attach the word "judgment" on the handle.

I looked for an appropriate jar, but was unable to find a mayonnaise jar or one of those frail jars that breaks easily. So my mother gave me a Mason jar, the kind ladies use for canning vegetables. Using adhesive tape, I attached the name "Christ" on the jar. The jar was heavy and durable; it could endure the heat of a pressure cooker at hundreds of degrees Fahrenheit. In my naiveté, I did not know the strength of the Mason jar. To me any glass jar was just another jar; and when a hammer hit the jar, it would break.

I went to the Five and Dime Store and selected a small, shiny figurine because it only cost 10 cents. It had the face of a Chinese lady. At home, I painted the small figurine jet black to show the blackness of sin.

The Disastrous Object Lesson

The following Sunday morning I introduced my object lesson by holding up the red hammer that had the word "judgment" taped on the handle. Bringing down the hammer from the sky, I explained to the children that God's judgment falls on all sin. Then walking over to a small table beside the pulpit, I pointed to my Chinese figurine painted jet black.

"For all have sinned, and come short of the glory of God," I quoted from Romans 3:23 (KJV).

Then pretending the hammer of God would fall on the jet-black sinner, I made a full roundhouse swing with the hammer, coming within inches of the figurine, but not smashing it.

"God's judgment should smash our sin," I explained to the children.

I repeated the roundhouse swing several times; the children in the front row were seated on the edge of the pew eager to see what I was doing. Two or three of them got off the pew and squatted to watch the red hammer come within inches of the jet-black Chinese figurine, which stood for sin.

"But Christ took our punishment for us," I explained to the children.

Then walking to the pulpit, I showed them the large jar on which I had taped the word "Christ." I placed the jet-black Chinese figurine within the large jar.

"On calvary we were placed in Christ and the judgment of God did not smash the figurine, but rather the judgment of God smashed Jesus Christ on calvary," I told the children.

I showed the children that the hammer would smash the jar, but not the jet-black figurine of the Chinese lady.

Standing in front of the children in Sunday School that day, I was unaware of the danger that lay ahead of me. If I had any idea what

Klunk. A louder sound echoed through the auditorium. The Mason jar did not break, and my ears began to turn red. Children began to laugh. In the back of the room the adults began to smile that knowing smile.

was going to happen, I would have stopped the demonstration right there. I would have explained what was going to happen, and not tried to break the jar.

In front of the children, I put the Mason jar on its side.

I explained to the children, "When the judgment of God—the hammer—falls on Christ, which is the Mason jar, we who are sinners are not harmed. The jar will be smashed because Christ took our penalty for us because we are in Christ—that is, in the jar. The figurine will not be hurt because the sinner will not be punished for his or her sin."

I swung the hammer to a full roundhouse circle, but not at full speed. As the hammer came close to the jar, I slowed the motion, expecting the hammer to crack and break the jar. Everyone heard it at the same time.

Klunk.

The hammer hit the jar, but the Mason jar did not break.

A few children chuckled because the jar had not broken.

I determined that the next time I would not slow down the hammer. I had announced that the judgment of God broke the jar and Christ would be crucified. So beginning my roundhouse swing again,

I brought the hammer down at the normal speed on the Mason jar.
KLUNK.

A louder sound echoed through the auditorium. The Mason jar did not break, and my ears began to turn red. Children began to laugh.

One child pointed at the jar, and said out loud, "It didn't break."

Several children put their hands to their mouths. In the back of the room the adults began to smile that knowing smile.

A Determined Last Swing

I was determined the next time would be the last time—next time the jar would break. So I retold the story of the judgment of God on sin. I replaced the jet-black Chinese figurine representing sin in the Mason jar. Placing the Mason jar on the small table, I took the red hammer and made a full roundhouse swing, twice as fast as I had earlier. I had no idea what would happen when I hit the thick walls of the Mason jar.

C...R...A...C...K. The glass splintered and the sound echoed throughout the auditorium. The splintered glass sprayed the children sitting in the front row.

"Y...E...E...E...Y...O...W," the children screamed in unison. Their hands flew to cover their faces and the audience erupted in panic.

I was stunned at what I had done, and was frozen with fear. My first reaction was that I had damaged some of the children's eyes.

Two or three mothers came running down the aisle, not caring that it was a church service. They panicked and ran to their children. The children kept screaming, crying and yelling; pandemonium broke out in the whole Sunday School assembly.

It took only a few minutes to determine that no one was hurt. When I think of the protective providence of God, I continue to pray daily for the Lord to "deliver [me] from the evil one" (Matt. 6:13). I thank God that on this occasion none of the splintered glass hit any of the children's eyes. No cuts or contusions resulted, and none of the children had been hit in the face with glass. Although they were peppered with glass splinters, we could see no obvious cuts.

The Humiliating Aftermath

Silla Hair suggested that we all go to our Sunday School classes. She volunteered to sweep up the glass and prepare the sanctuary for the morning service.

I shook to the core. In front of all these people I had done an immature thing. I had appeared foolish, and everyone knew it.

I do not remember anything about my Sunday School lesson to the junior boys that day. I remember being so shook up that I could barely present the lesson.

At 11:00 A.M. I had to preach, and again I was still upset by the immature act I had performed in the Sunday School assembly. Again, I do not remember what I preached about, but somehow I struggled through the sermon and the rest of the worship service.

I learned my lesson that Sunday, and decided to dispense with object lessons. Because of the many compliments I had previously received about my "special effects" during the Sunday School assembly, I thought I had to top off each Sunday with a better, bigger show. I realized my motives were wrong after my big fiasco of the shattered glass jar.

PRINCIPLES TO TAKE AWAY

1. *The principle of expressing, not impressing.* I wanted my superintendent's devotional to have a spiritual influence on people, but I was always tempted to entertain or be impressive rather than to explain the Word of God. A minister must try to be expressive, not impressive. As I look back at the broken jar lesson, I realize that sometimes a minister is blinded to the purposes of his heart. Whereas he may think his motives are absolutely pure in serving Christ, sometimes the motives are self-supporting and he is feeding his own ego while serving the Lord.

2. *The principle of "the show must go on."* The world uses the expression "the show must go on," and this also applies to those of us who preach sermons: The sermon must go on. Because I embarrassed myself by shattering the glass jar, I was unable to adequately teach a Sunday School lesson or preach a sermon. Every minister makes mistakes, but must immediately walk away from the mistakes and continue serving the Lord. My mistake was so wrapped up in ego, however, that I was not able to forget it. In my heart I knew I was "showing off" while presenting a gospel message. If my motives had been right, I would not have cared what people thought about me.

"Herb Dickinson replaced the 'Preacher'"

19

Becoming Baptist

I eagerly reached into the mailbox and pulled out the cream-colored envelope. Its return address was Fuller Theological Seminary. I knew this was the acceptance into seminary I had eagerly awaited.

Fuller Theological Seminary was the hottest seminary in the evangelical world; it was attracting the greatest Christian scholars from throughout the world. Because it was considered the best, everyone wanted to attend Fuller. Because it was the best, I also wanted to attend Fuller Seminary; it was the only one I considered.

"We regret to inform you," my countenance dropped as I read the letter, "your application has been denied because Columbia Bible College is not accredited, nor recognized..."

My vision of attending the best seminary collapsed right there in front of the student mailboxes at Columbia Bible College. I had one more year of college left. I had planned that year carefully. I planned to continue pastoring Westminster Presbyterian Church for one more year, then move to California to attend Fuller.

I discovered that when God shuts one door, He usually opens another. My father-in-law, Mr. E. B. Forbes, a Christian contractor in St. Louis, Missouri, told me I should transfer immediately to Northwestern College in Minneapolis, Minnesota. Billy Graham was president of Northwestern, and I could graduate in one year at the accredited college, then enter Fuller Theological Seminary.

Leaving Westminster Presbyterian Church

The following weekend I broke the news about my plans to leave to the five ladies at Westminster Presbyterian Church. Then I shared it with the two elders. I persuaded them that Herb Dickinson, my friend at Columbia Bible College, would be an outstanding pastor to replace me. So they called Herb to pastor the church and I moved to Minnesota to attend Northwestern College.

From Policeman to Pastor

Herb Dickinson came to the church, but only stayed three months because his schedule became too hectic. So Herb released the responsibilities of the church to a Chatham County policeman who attended Westminster Presbyterian church. Starting in 1954, the policeman pastored the church as a laypastor for more than a year. Although he was dedicated to hospital visitation and soul winning, he was weak in the pulpit; but of course he was not trained in that area.

I met the policeman when he first visited Westminster Presbyterian Church. He came as a result of revival in the community. He grew up in West Savannah and attended the church as a teenager, but was not sure of his salvation. During one of my sermons he was convicted of sin, walked down the aisle at the invitation and knelt at the altar to make his life right with God.

The policeman, like Paul on the road to Damascus, instantly turned from darkness to light. God gave him a burden for souls and he went door-to-door with me to win people to Christ.

I preached every Thursday at the Union Mission, a downtown Savannah rescue mission for homeless men. I took the policeman with me to share his testimony. He went back with me every Thursday to share Christ with the men. Within a few months he was preaching at the Union Mission weekly. When I went to St. Louis, Missouri, to be married on August 21, 1953, the policeman preached the morning and evening services at Westminster Presbyterian Church while I was gone. It was his first sermon in a church, although he had preached at the rescue mission.

Although the policeman was faithful in ministry, he did not have the "spark" in the pulpit to attract large crowds. He was faithful in presenting the gospel, but people did not walk the aisle to be saved. The people missed the evangelistic fire they were used to. As a pastor, the policeman could not hold the audience's attention and attendance began to decline. New members did not replace the people who moved out of the community. Soon church attendance declined from more than 100 to less than 50 people.

The Power of the Baptist Preacher

Cecil Hodges, a young Baptist preacher, became pastor of the newly established Bible Baptist Church. Cecil, a charismatic personality who had the anointing of God upon his ministry, led the Bible Baptist Church in explosive growth, as rapidly as the former growth of Westminster Presbyterian Church.

The Bible Baptist Church building was not attractive. When Cecil Hodges first came, the building was a simple rectangular structure and had only a dirt floor. The first thing the new pastor did was to pour a concrete floor. The greatness of this crude little building was the powerful preaching of its new preacher.

After Cecil Hodges became established at the Baptist church, the policeman asked him to preach a weekend revival meeting on Friday and Saturday night at Westminster Presbyterian Church. The five ladies who had called me as pastor became excited about revival. They visited door-to-door inviting everyone, and as a result the little Presbyterian Church was filled on Friday night, the first night of the revival meetings. Cecil Hodges preached a powerful sermon, and more than 25 people came forward to be saved.

The next night the crowd was even larger; people were standing against the walls. Again Cecil preached a powerful message, and again more than 25 people came forward to be saved. After the people had been led to Christ, Cecil asked the converts to stand in front of the pulpit, just as he did in the Baptist church. The large group of converts stretched from the piano to the outer wall.

A Question of Baptism

Pastor Hodges asked the new converts, "When are you people going to get baptized?"

"We'll get Reverend Carroll Stegall to come and sprinkle them," one of the five ladies answered from the pews.

The people in West Savannah were used to speaking up in the church service.

"No," Cecil answered the lady, reaching for his Bible. "I mean when are you going to baptize them by immersion like the Bible commands?"

Pastor Hodges turned to the story of the Ethiopian eunuch, showing how he was immersed immediately after conversion. Then turning the pages of the New Testament, from illustration to illustration, Hodges showed how all new Christians in the Bible were immediately baptized.

Then directing his question to the people standing in front of him, Hodges again asked, "Do you want to obey God and be baptized?"

"Yes," they answered in unison.

Hodges invited them to attend the Bible Baptist Church the following evening, which was Sunday night. He gave directions to the church and promised them a Bible message about baptism.

"It will be a Bible study about baptism, not a sermon," he explained.

A Sunday Evening Phenomena at Bible Baptist Church

Sunday morning the policeman preached at Westminster Presbyterian Church, and announced that the evening service would be held at Bible Baptist Church. He also gave the directions to the church. Many of those in attendance that morning planned to go and hear Pastor Hodges that evening.

About 50 people from the Presbyterian Church attended the Baptist Church to hear Pastor Hodges that Sunday evening. Not all the 50 people who had come forward to be saved were there; only about half of them came. About half of the regular attenders from the little Presbyterian Church, however, visited the Baptist Church that evening. The Bible Baptist Church was packed and the building was hot.

"This is the largest Sunday evening crowd we have ever had," Pastor Hodges announced to those gathered in the concrete-block building.

Then taking his Bible, Hodges turned from Scripture to Scripture, explaining the necessity of being baptized by immersion. To his credit, he never said sprinkling was wrong, nor did he attack the Presbyterian way of baptizing. Hodges simply taught what he believed about baptism from the Bible, and asked the people to read what the Bible said.

The Presbyterians Became Baptists Through Baptism
Then Hodges gave a gospel invitation.

"I want you to come forward as a candidate to be scripturally baptized tonight," Cecil invited people to walk an aisle as candidates for baptism by immersion.

When the Presbyterians from Westminster were immersed in the Baptist church, they were doing more than following the Lord in baptism—they were becoming members of the Bible Baptist Church.

Cecil Hodges believed that immersion also meant church membership. To him, baptism was the doorway into the Baptist church. When the Presbyterians from Westminster were immersed in the Baptist church, they were doing more than following the Lord in baptism—they were becoming members of the Bible Baptist Church.

Not all the Presbyterians went forward that evening, but many of them did, including most of the five ladies who had originally called me to pastor the church. Many were baptized that evening in the church's small baptistery; a few put it off until succeeding weeks for one reason or another.

One said, "I want my husband here to be baptized with me."

The Demise of Westminster Presbyterian Church
That evening Cecil Hodges functionally shut down Westminster Presbyterian Church, although the next two weeks the policeman continued to conduct Sunday School and church services. The Presbyterian crowd was small and the leadership was gone. The policeman resigned

and the Independent Presbyterian Church shut down the Westminster Presbyterian Church of West Savannah. (Today, another Westminster Presbyterian Church functions in Savannah, but it is not the same continuing congregation, nor does it occupy the same building.)

"Let's Don't Become Baptist"

The month the Presbyterians of West Savannah became Baptists, the same thing was symbolically happening to me one thousand miles away in Dallas, Texas.

I had done everything possible to enter Fuller Theological Seminary, but enrolled instead at Dallas Theological Seminary in Dallas, Texas.

When my wife and I arrived in Dallas, we visited three or four Presbyterian churches, looking for a congregation that had the evangelistic zeal of Westminster Presbyterian Church in Savannah, Georgia. We could not find a Presbyterian church, however, that was exciting, evangelistic and offered motivating preaching.

One Sunday evening we visited First Baptist Church in downtown Dallas because a symphony orchestra played special music that night. After my wife and I arrived home that evening, she had a life-threatening emergency and was taken to the Baptist Hospital in the middle of the night. She needed surgery to save her life.

When I was checking my wife into the hospital, the nurse filling out the registration papers asked an innocent question, "What is your church home?"

"We don't have one yet," I answered.

"Where did you attend church today?"

"First Baptist Church in downtown Dallas," I answered.

I did not think anything about the conversation, but the nurse entered First Baptist Church as our church home. After surgery I was allowed into the postoperative recovery room to see my wife. Dr. Schaffer, visitation pastor of First Baptist Church, was standing there talking to her.

"I understand you kids don't have any money to take care of your bill," Dr. Schaffer said to me.

"The First Baptist Church will help you," he advised.

When I arrived home that evening at approximately six o'clock, a couple was sitting in a car at the curb outside our duplex. The man introduced himself as the teacher of the Young Married Couples

Class at First Baptist, where we had been assigned. The woman had brought a casserole for dinner. When we went into the duplex she made the beds, cleaned the kitchen and together we sat down to eat the casserole they had brought.

"Tomorrow night somebody else from the class will be here with dinner," they said before leaving.

My wife and I were tremendously impressed with the friendliness and personal ministry of First Baptist Church; but more than that, we were amazed at the evangelistic outreach of one of the largest churches in America. Yet this big church could help one couple who had visited the church.

"Let's attend First Baptist Church and learn the spirit of this great church," I told my wife.

Then I added, "Let's don't become Baptist."

Changing My Views from Sprinkling to Immersion

Beginning in 1944, Pastor W. A. Criswell of First Baptist Church preached verse by verse through the whole Bible from Genesis 1:1 to Revelation 22:21. From 1954 to 1955 we heard preaching from Romans 4 to 1 Corinthians 1 at the church.

When Dr. Criswell came to Romans 6, he read verses 3-6 *(KJV)*:

> Know ye not, that so many of us as were baptized into Jesus Christ were baptized into his death?
>
> Therefore we are buried with him by baptism into death: that like as Christ was raised up from the dead by the glory of the Father, even so we also should walk in newness of life.
>
> For if we have been planted together in the likeness of his death, we shall be also in the likeness of his resurrection:
>
> Knowing this, that our old man is crucified with him, that the body of sin might be destroyed, that henceforth we should not serve sin.

"Tonight I am going to preach on baptism," Dr. Criswell said.

Then with a twinkle in his eye, Dr. Criswell told the audience, "There is no water baptism in Romans 6."

That evening I came to the church and sat right in the middle of the congregation holding my Greek New Testament. I wanted to compare

Dr. Criswell's words to the biblical text. I did not want to argue, I just wanted to see if he could properly interpret the biblical view of baptism. I was convinced that baptism by sprinkling was correct.

Back at Columbia Bible College, I had argued the mode of baptism with other students, passionately defending baptism by sprinkling. That evening Dr. Criswell began his sermon by repeating what he had said that morning.

"There is no water baptism in Romans, chapter 6."

That evening, Elmer Towns the Presbyterian died. Although I would respect my Presbyterian roots, and love my Presbyterian mother, from that moment on I would never again be Presbyterian.

Amen, I said in my heart, fondly stroking my Greek New Testament.

"When Jesus died on the cross, you were placed in Christ," Dr. Criswell made his first point. He went on to say that to be identified with Christ was spiritual baptism, not water baptism.

Amen, I agreed.

"When Jesus was crucified on the cross, you were crucified with Him," Dr. Criswell proclaimed.

Amen, I agreed.

"When Jesus was buried in the grave, you were buried with Him," Dr. Criswell preached.

Amen, I agreed.

"When Jesus was raised from the dead, you were in Christ being raised from the dead with Him," Dr. Criswell maintained.

Amen, I agreed.

The analogy of our being placed into Christ was repeated by Dr. Criswell several times, if not a dozen times. Each time he repeated the fact that this baptism was spiritual baptism, not water baptism, I could only agree.

Amen, I agreed.

"If..." Dr. Criswell lifted his voice to his highest apex.

"If..." Dr. Criswell repeated himself again, louder.

"If you have been identified with Christ in His death, if you have been identified with Christ in His burial, if you have been identified with Christ in His resurrection, why not tell the world by water symbolism?"

Like a crisis decision that must be made immediately, I changed my entire view of baptism instantaneously. What he said made sense. My spirit agreed with his view of water baptism.

Amen, I agreed.

That evening, Elmer Towns the Presbyterian died. Although I would respect my Presbyterian roots, and love my Presbyterian mother, from that moment on I would never again be Presbyterian.

At Columbia Bible College I had heard all the arguments for baptism by immersion from my classmates. I was able to answer all their arguments; but when faced with great passionate preaching tied to biblical exegesis, I moved from the world of sprinkling into the world of immersion. I became a Baptist.

The "Preacher" and His Presbyterians Henceforth Were Baptists

My greatest allegiance, however, is not to the Baptist church, but to the Body of Christ. I love those who love Christ and identify with those who take up His cross and follow Him, regardless of their church affiliation.

A thousand miles away, Westminster Presbyterian Church was experiencing a similar change. Many of those I had led to Christ were becoming Baptists. Cecil Hodges was immersing people into Bible Baptist Church and they would henceforth be Baptists.

In Dallas, Texas, the one who had led the people from Westminster Presbyterian Church to Christ also was making that change. From henceforth he would be Baptist.

PRINCIPLES TO TAKE AWAY

1. *The principle of enlightened passion.* Arguments or reasons do not change people's minds, nor does correct rhetoric

make a difference. A combination of biblically based arguments presented with passion changes people's thinking.

2. *The principle of anointed preaching.* The policeman who became the pastor of Westminster Presbyterian Church believed in the right doctrine and was yielded to Christ, but his preaching did not have an anointing from God. Because of this, attendance declined in the church. When an anointed preacher visited the church, although he had a different denominational persuasion, the people responded to his preaching. The church experienced revival and Cecil Hodges built a great church because the Holy Spirit anointed his preaching.

3. *The remnant principle.* A group of God's people, no matter how small, will always be true to Him. Although the policeman was not an anointed preacher, a remnant at the church remained true to God.

4. *The principle of sovereign design.* I believe God wanted me at Dallas Theological Seminary, although I did everything I could to enter Fuller Theological Seminary. Today, I am a dispensationalist and reflect the theology of Dallas Seminary. If I had not attended Dallas Seminary, I would not have received the solid grounding in theology to complement my Presbyterian roots, thus providing a balanced view of ministry. Dallas Seminary was imperative for me during the 1950s, and I am glad I did not attend Fuller for my basic seminary training. God heard my prayer, however, and I graduated from Fuller Theological Seminary 25 years later and earned my doctorate degree.

5. *The principle of following one's heart.* Although I was not seeking to become a Baptist nor was I studying the Baptist position, I simply was following my heart when I changed from Presbyterian to Baptist beliefs. I believe a scholarly argument could not have changed my convictions, but Dr. W. A. Criswell touched my heart with anointed preaching and scholarly exegesis.

6. *The principle of my lifelong love affair with large churches.* Several years later I wrote the book *The Ten Largest Sunday Schools and What Made Them Grow* (Baker Book House, 1969). This book became a best-seller and, according to C. Peter Wagner of Fuller Theological Seminary, it was the first book about the megachurches of America and the first

American church-growth book. This book would never have been written if I had never fallen in love with the large First Baptist Church in Dallas, Texas. I loved the church, not because of its size, but because of how they took care of one couple who visited its services. When I later tried to communicate the effectiveness of large churches, it was not from a scholarly perspective, but from the heart.

7. *The principle of choice.* I have always been intrigued with the way people make choices and arrive at decisions. Some choices are made because of intellectual knowledge, others because of heartfelt emotions. Some people make choices because of their backgrounds, presuppositions or for many other reasons. Often I am asked why I left the Presbyterian church to become a Baptist. I do not always provide a theological answer. I was following my heart in that change. At the time, I did not realize Baptist churches were more evangelistically oriented than were Presbyterian churches. Yet that is what I was seeking. I also did not realize that at the time Baptist churches were more "user friendly" in their commitment to congregational government and involving everyone in ministry. I made a choice on my knees because I believed God wanted me to change. What I did, I did because God led me.

"Dr. W. A. Criswell and me, as Dr. Towns"

"Me and Ruth on wedding day—August 21, 1953"

Epilogue

I love the church, which means I love to attend church services, I love to serve in the church, I love to pray for the church and I love to give money to the church. I love to reach people for Christ through the church. I love to fellowship with Christians in the church. I love the Church because it is the Body of Christ (see Eph. 1:22,23), and I love Jesus Christ. He has saved me, called me to full-time service and given meaning to my life.

Because of my love for Jesus Christ, I jumped on my bicycle to ride all around Savannah, Georgia, telling people they needed "to be born again." I did whatever was necessary, visiting wayward members, praying for the sick, gathering crowds and organizing workers.

When you love others, you cry and suffer pain when they hurt. I agonized with every failure at Westminster Presbyterian Church and wept while battling the former elders for leadership.

When you love others, you smile and laugh at their victories. I delighted when the people painted the whole church in a whole day. I was happily affirmed by each victory.

When you love others, you identify with their dreams and aspirations. Their hopes become your future. I wanted Westminster Presbyterian Church to grow, buy property and construct new buildings. The future of Westminster Presbyterian Church was my future. I planned to stay there the rest of my life, and would have, except God moved me on in geography and understanding.

God has promised, "I will pour out My Spirit"; so we define atmospheric revival as "the presence of God among His people." While I was at Westminster Presbyterian Church, the church experienced continual revival. I felt God's presence in the church services. I felt Him because He WAS there. The good people of West Savannah yielded themselves to be filled by His presence and God moved through the neighborhood. So I loved Westminster Presbyterian Church because I love Jesus Christ, who lives in the church and is the Church.

More Timely Wisdom from Elmer Towns

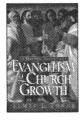

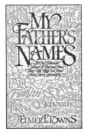

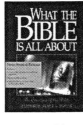